AutoCAD 2007

2D Mechanical Design

Frede Uhrskov

Preface

The tutorials in this booklet are made for new users in the mechanic area.

The tutorials are made as step-by-step. I have made them in that way because I want the user getting success as soon as possible.

I hope you will enjoy the tutorials and that you will be a better constructor using AutoCAD.

The tutorials are all made in metric.

If you want me to change anything about the tutorials – feel free to contact me at the email below.

frede@uhrskov.com.

Good luck

Denmark 2006

Frede Uhrskov

Directory

Read this first

It is strongly recommended that:

- AutoCAD is correctly installed
- You use AutoCAD with the standard layout and without any change of the toolbars.
- You know how to make a projected drawing for the mechanical industry.

The layers in the drawing are layers, that I use in my drawing and you can change their names as you like.

Block of iron

The objective of the tutorial

The objective of the tutorial is to make a block as you se below. It is shown isometric, but we will make the drawings in 3 projection planes, so they can be used when you have to make the block in practice.

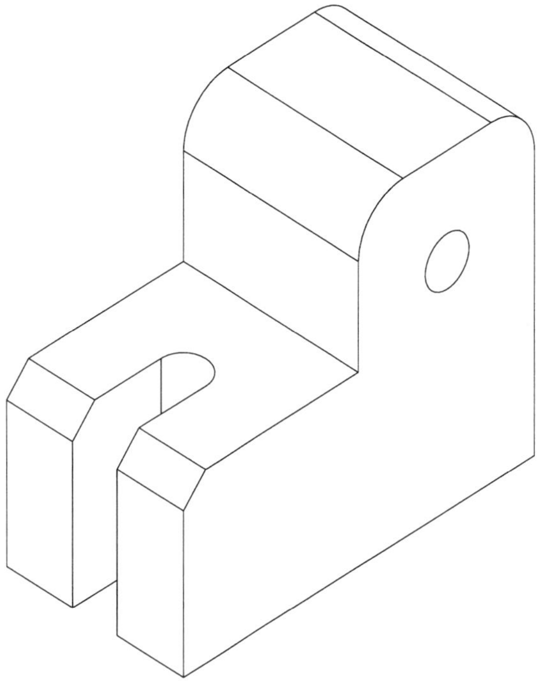

Making layers

Exercise 01 - LAYER

First you have to make layers with different names - I made the layers showed in this table:

Layers			
Name	Color	Linetype	Lineweight
Frame	Yellow	Continuous	0,5
Midline	Red	Center	0,25
Dimension	Red	Continuous	0,25
Hatch	Green	Continuous	0,25
Hidden line	Green	Hidden	0,25
Section line	Red	Center	0,25
Text	Magenta	Continuous	0,35

You can do it in this way:

- Click the shown button

A dialog is shown:

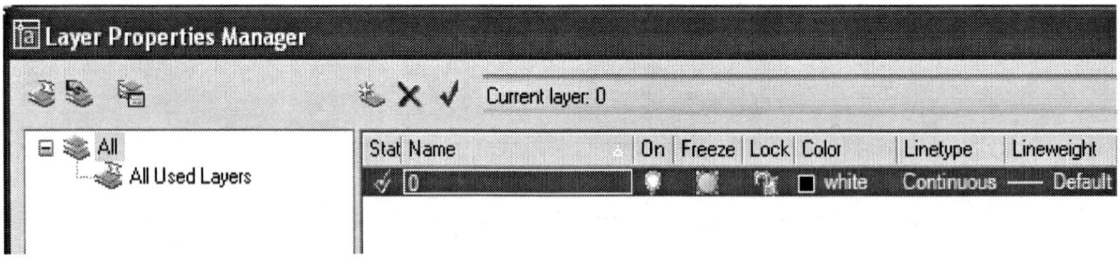

Click New Layer 

A new layer called **Layer1** is made

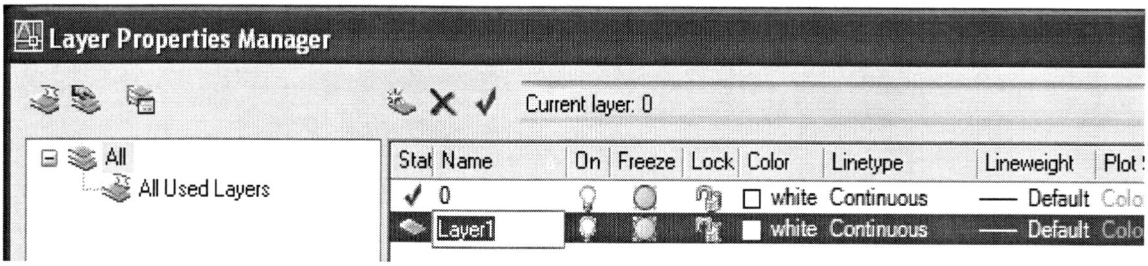

Write the name of the layer in the blue box. Note, that the marked text disappears, when you start writing.

Hit ENTER when you have finished writing the name of the layer.

Change the color of the layer by clicking the name of the color.

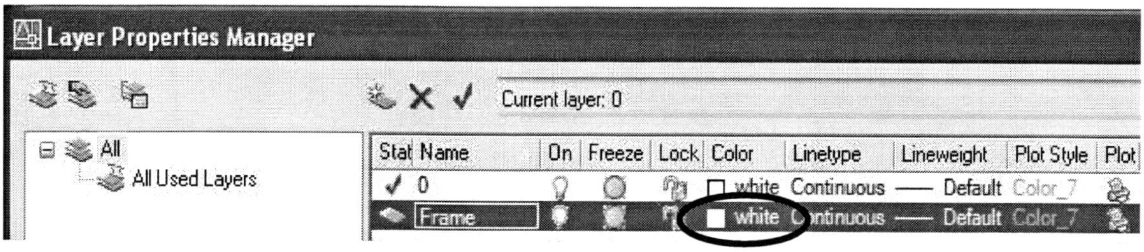

The color dialog shows and you can choose the color you want.

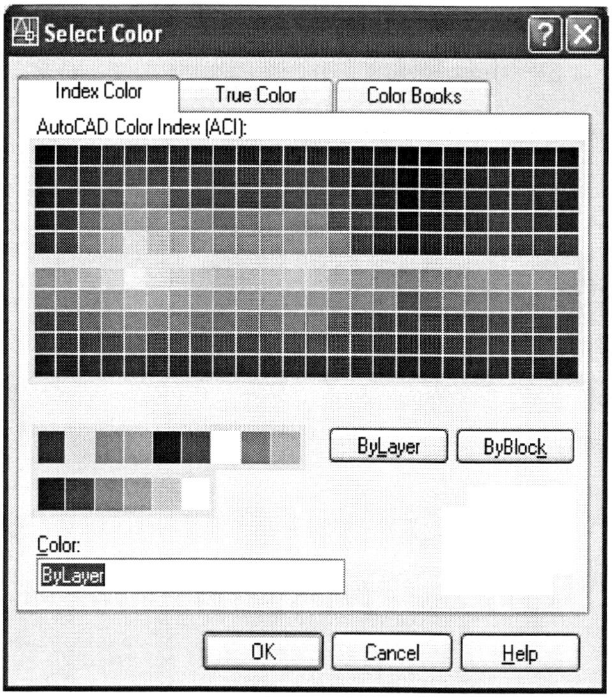

The line type of the layer is set by clicking the name **Continuous**:

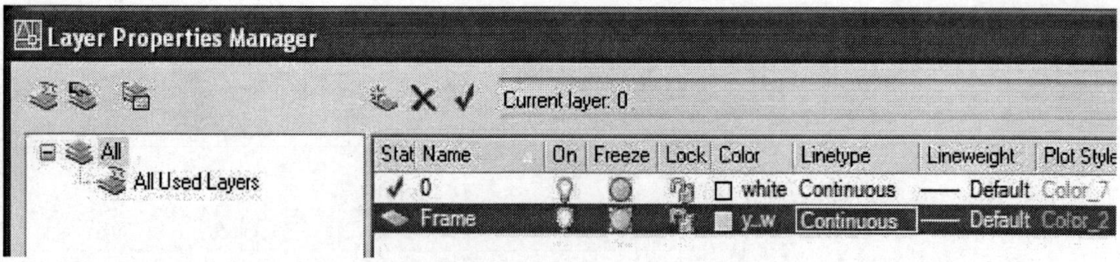

A dialog shows the line types already loaded.

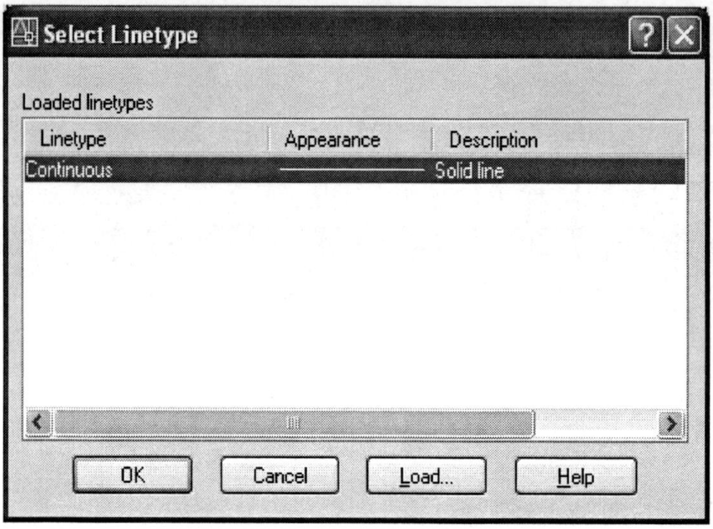

As you can see only one line type is loaded at this time.

The other line types have to be loaded into the drawing.

Click **Load…** 

In this dialog you can choose a specific line type or you can choose them all

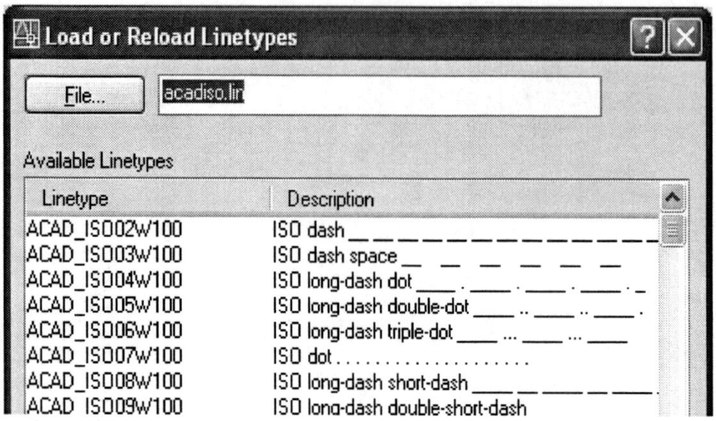

If you want to load all the line types, you can use **Ctrl+A**
All the line types will then be marked and you can hit **OK**

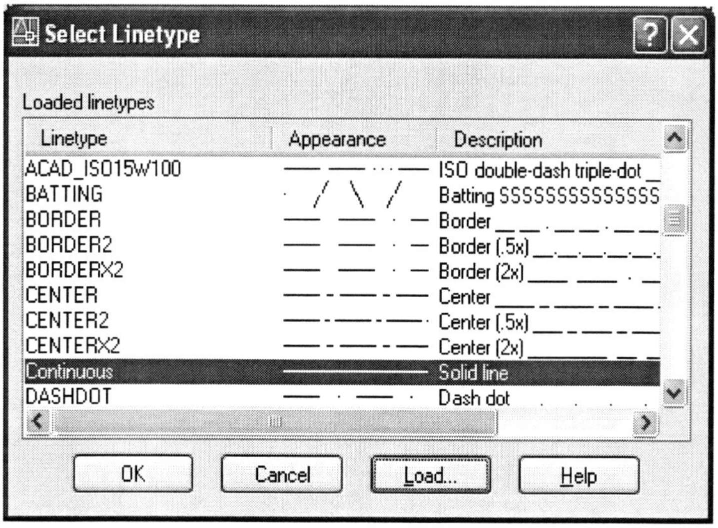

Now you will return to the prior dialog and you can choose the line type that you want for the layer you just created.

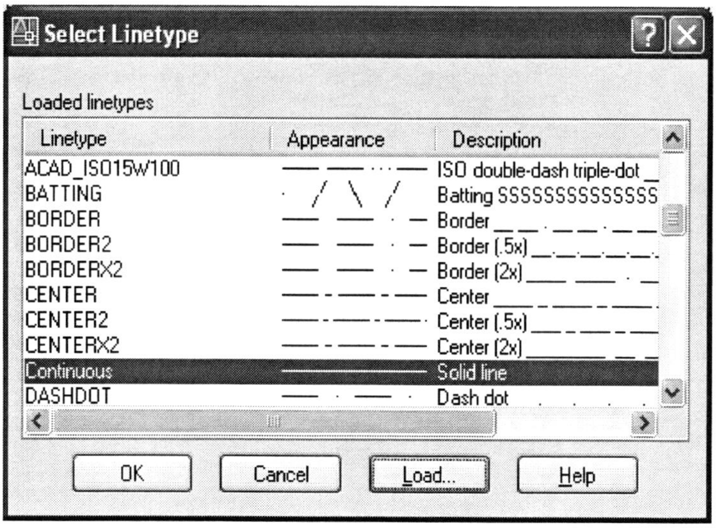

Make the layers in the table and give them the colors and line type as shown.

Template

If you want to reuse the layers, you can save the drawing as a template, which is a standard drawing.

Use the **Save** As and choose the file type DWT see the pictures below.

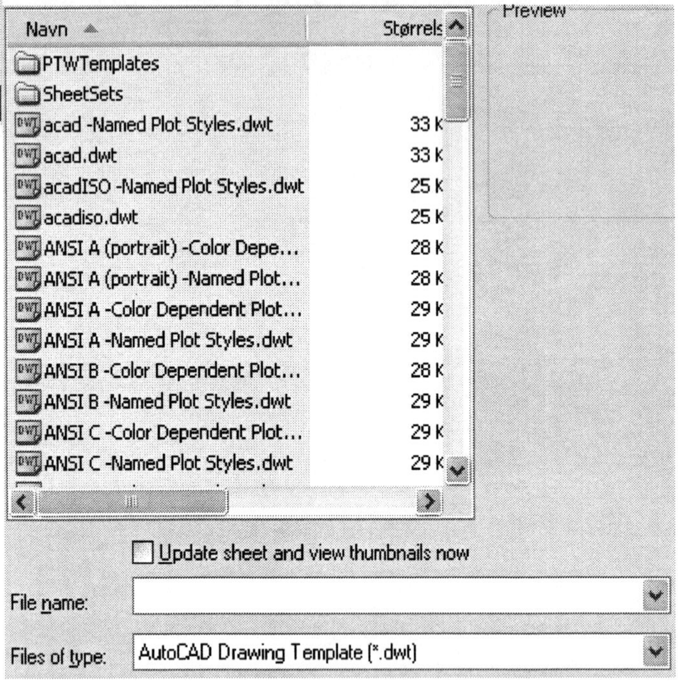

Block of iron

Now we are going to draw a block with a hole, a bend, a chamfer and a milled part.

The drawing should look like this at the end.

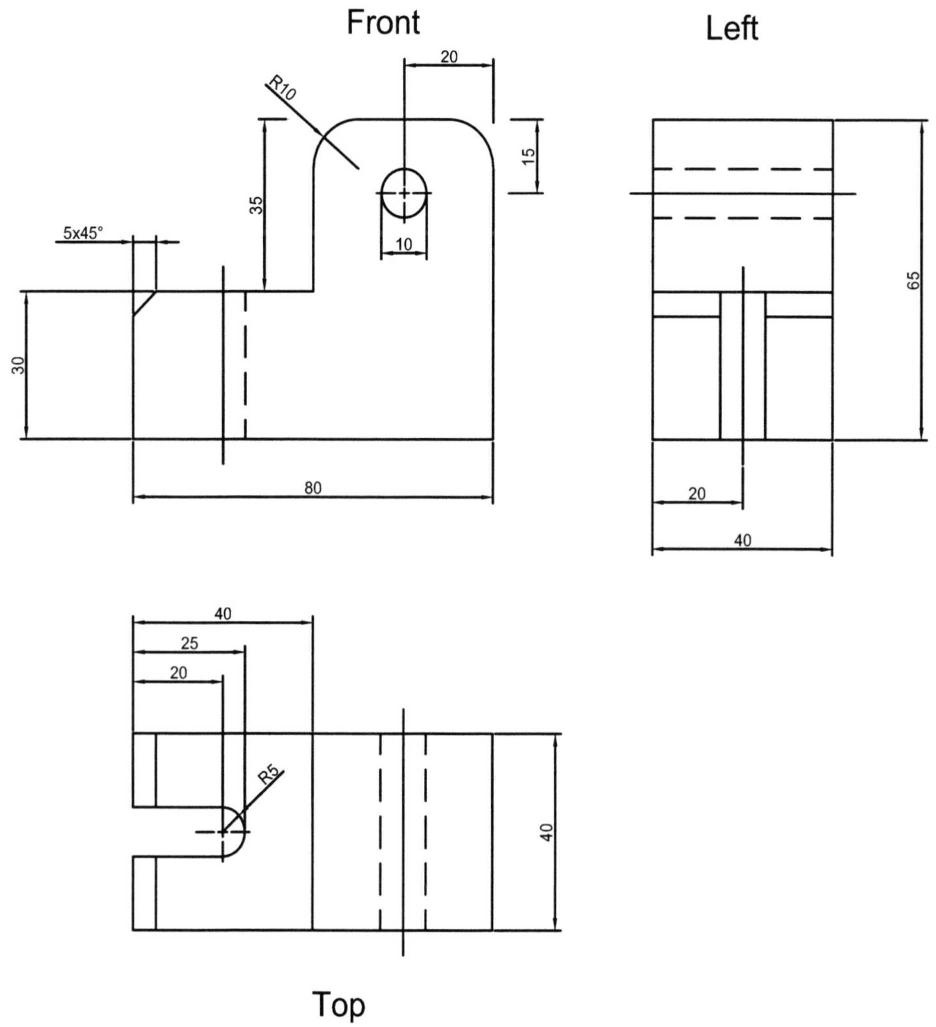

Drawing the frame

Exercise 02 - Line

New layer

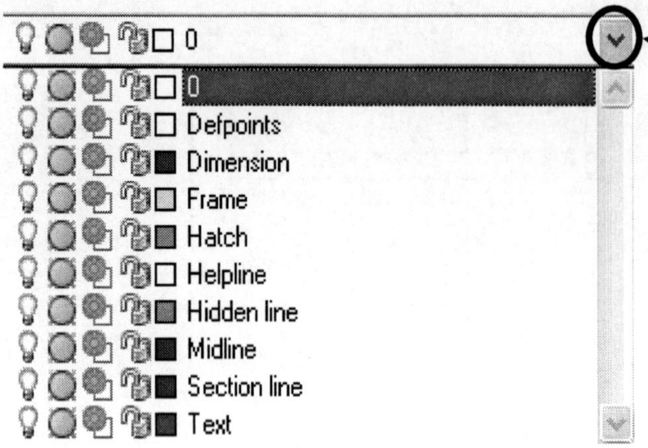

1) Hit the drop down arrow

2) Choose **Frame**

3) Choose **LINE**

4) Select a point on the screen, where you want the line to start – that is point 1

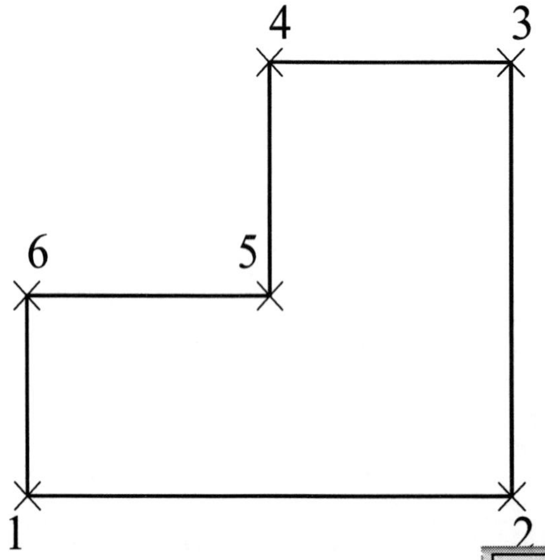

5) Activate the button **POLAR** 

6) Move the cursor in the direction of point 2 – be sure that you see the broken line on the screen. That indicates a horizontal line.

7) Type 80 ENTER

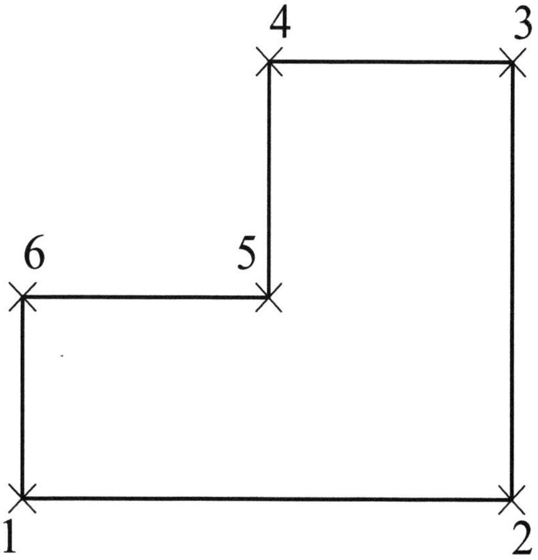

8) Move the cursor in the direction of point 3

9) Type 65 ENTER

10) Move the cursor in the direction of point 4

11) Type 40 ENTER

12) Move the cursor in the direction of point 5

13) Type 35 ENTER

14) Move the cursor in the direction of point 6

15) Type 40 ENTER

16) Type C for Close

Now you are going to draw the hidden lines.

1) Change the layer to **HIDDEN**

2) Choose **LINE** (Type L)

3) Activate **POLAR** 

4) Keep the cursor still on point 1 – don't click

5) Move the cursor to the right – be sure that you see the POLAR line

6) Type 15 ENTER

7) The start point for the next line is now placed 15 mm. from point 1

8) Choose OSNAP PERP 

9) Click at the opposite line – between point 5 and 6

10) Hit ENTER to end drawing the line

Drawing the second hidden line

11) Choose LINE

12) Keep the cursor still on the endpoint of the first hidden line – don't click

13) Move the cursor to the right – be sure that you see the POLAR line

14) Type 10 ENTER

15) The start point for the second line is now placed 10 mm. from the endpoint of the first hidden line

16) Choose **OSNAP PERP**

17) Click at the opposite line – between point 5 and 6

18) Hit ENTER to end drawing lines

Drawing the centre line between the 2 hidden lines

1) Change LAYER to MIDLINE

2) Choose LINE

3) Choose OSNAP FROM

4) Choose OSNAP END

5) Pick the lower endpoint of the right hidden line

6) Type @-5,-5 ENTER

7) The start point of the midline is now placed 5 mm. below the horizontal line

8) Move the cursor vertical so you can see the polar line

9) Type 40 ENTER - ENTER

The drawing should look like this:

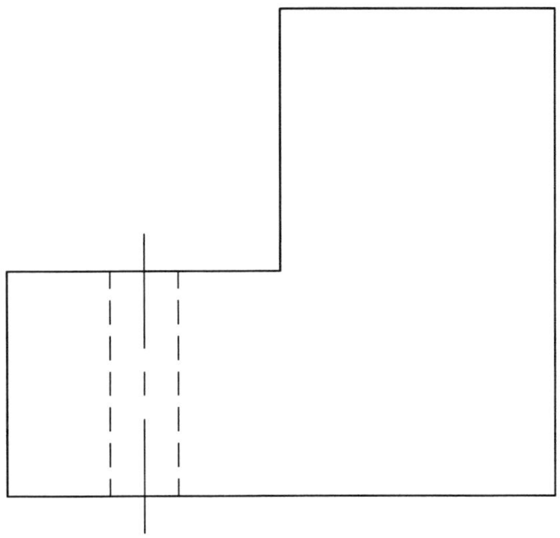

If the HIDDEN lines don't shows as hidden you can adjust the spaces between the lines with the command LTSCALE.
Type LTSCALE and set the value to a different value – default is 1 – and you maybe need to try different values before you are satisfied. I prefer a distance about 0.25.

Save the drawing to the disk.

Exercise 03 - Line

We are now going to draw the block from the top and from the left.

1) Change to the layer FRAME

2) Chose LINE

3) Keep the cursor still at the lower left corner of the drawing as shown on the picture – point 1

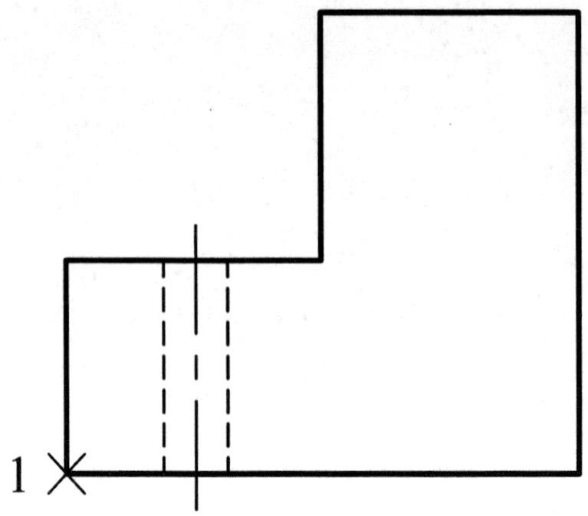

4) Move the cursor down and vertical so you see the polar line

5) Type 40 ENTER

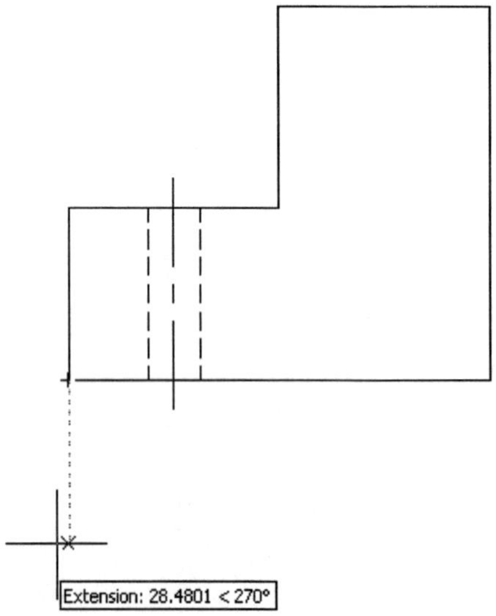

Now the start point for the first line in the TOP picture is placed 40 mm. below the FRONT picture.

- Move the cursor to the lower right corner of the front view. Hold the cursor still in a moment until you see a little cross in the middle of the cursor.

- Move the cursor down, so you see the polar line.

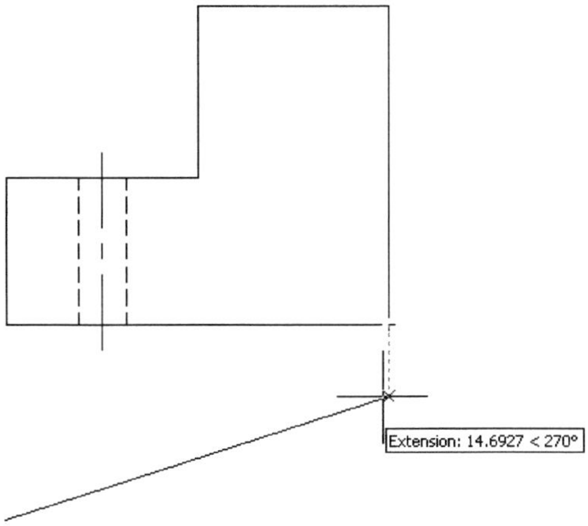

- Move the polar line until the vertical and the horizontal line snaps together.

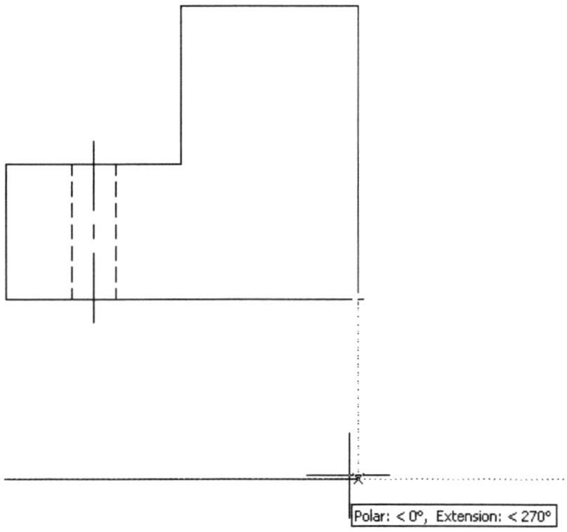

- Click the left button on the mouse and the line is drawn.

- Move the cursor down and type 40 ENTER

- Move the cursor to the left and type 80 ENTER

- Type C for Close or connect the line with the cursor. If you connect the lines by clicking the mouse, you have to end the command with ENTER.

- Draw in the same way the view LEFT

The drawing should look like this:

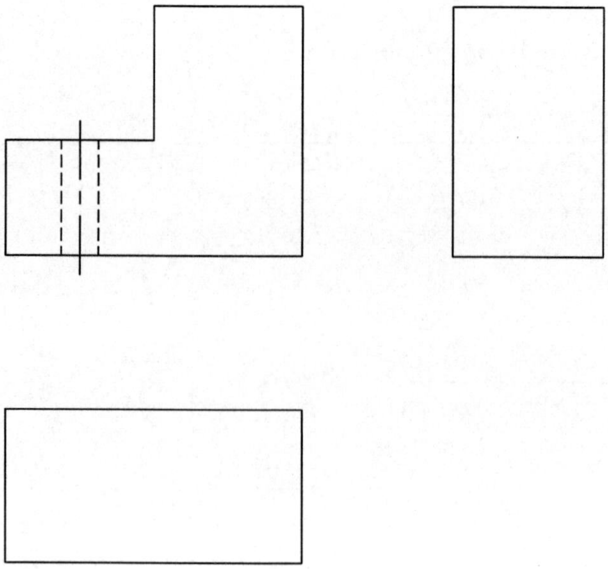

- Choose LINE
- Keep the cursor still for a moment by point 1 and draw the polar line to point 2 – the cursor will snap to the intersection point on the line.

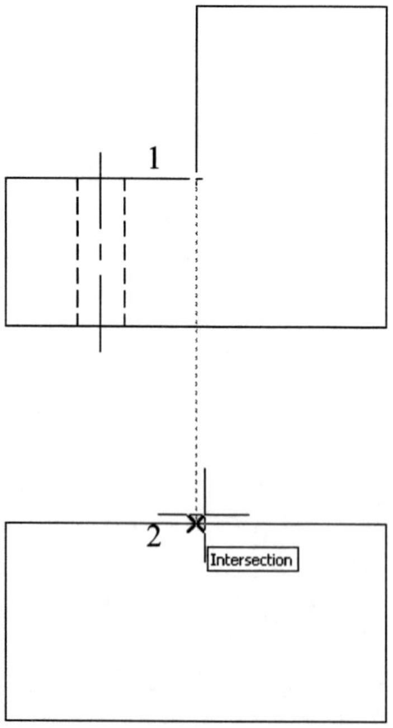

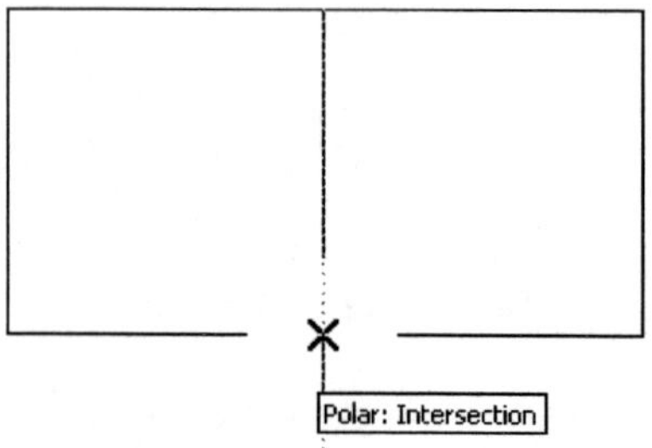

- Click at the point and draw the line to the opposite line – like the illustration to the right.
- Save the drawing

- Use the same technique to draw the horizontal line in the view LEFT

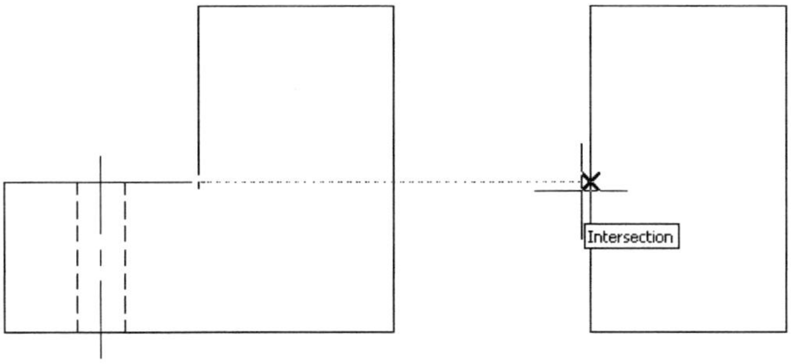

The drawing should now look like this:

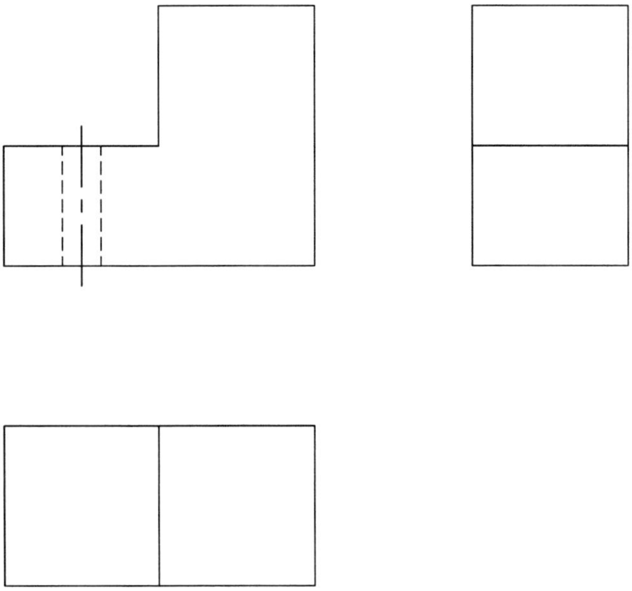

Objektsnap

When you are working with drawings in AutoCAD it is very important that the objects snaps together in the points you wish. The OSNAP command is the tool doing this.

You can use OSNAP permanent – running OSNAP or you can use it temporary is time you need it.

In the next tutorial, we will use OSNAP permanent.

Exercise 04 - DDOSNAP

- Type OS for OSNAP
- Mark the shown snaps

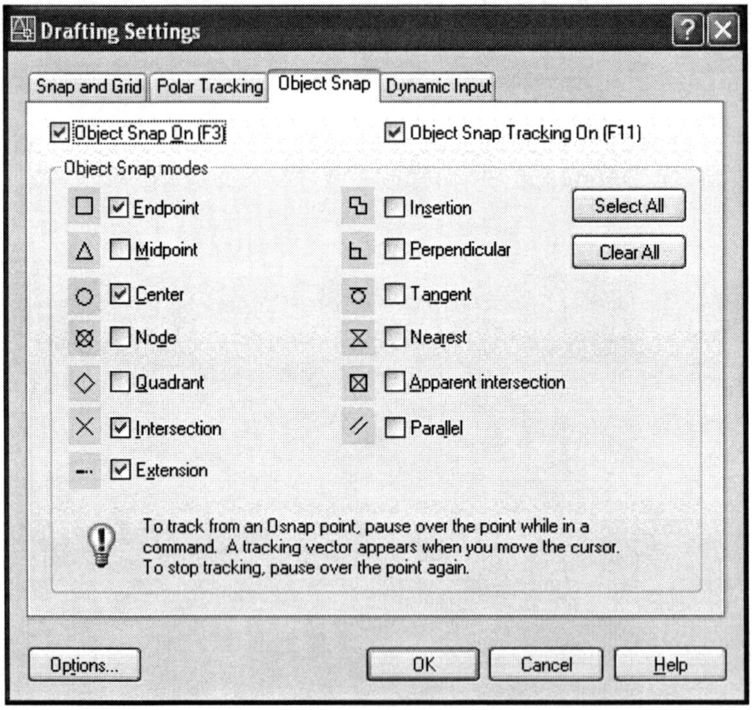

Exercise 05 - Circles

- You need to have this drawing on your screen.

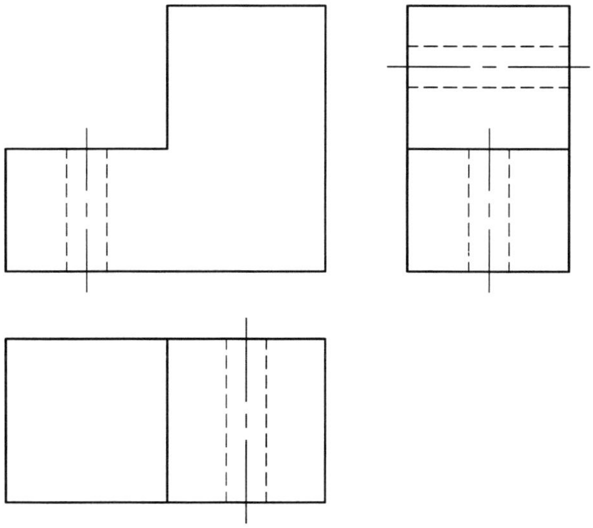

- Change the layer to FRAME
- Choose CIRCLE 
- Choose OSNAP - FROM 
- Chose OSNAP END 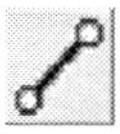
- Click the upper left corner in the view FRONT
- Key in @20,-15
- Key in the radius of the circle – 5
- Use the same method to draw the circle in the view TOP

Your drawing should look like this:

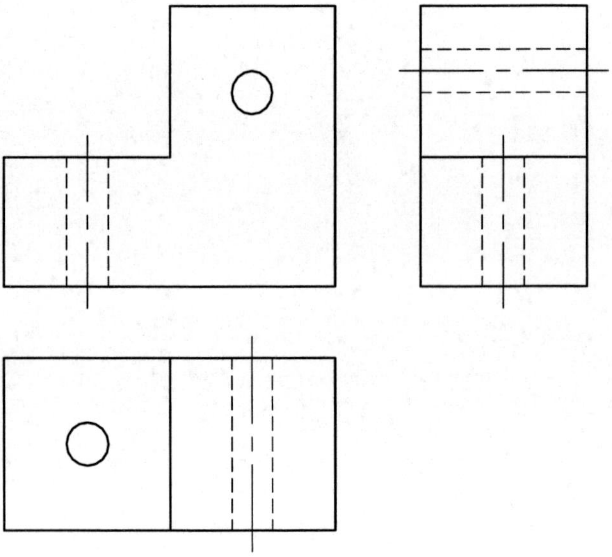

- Save the drawing

Centreline

The circles have to be shown with centre lines – we can draw those using the dimension menu.

Exercise 06 - DDIM

- Key in DDIM

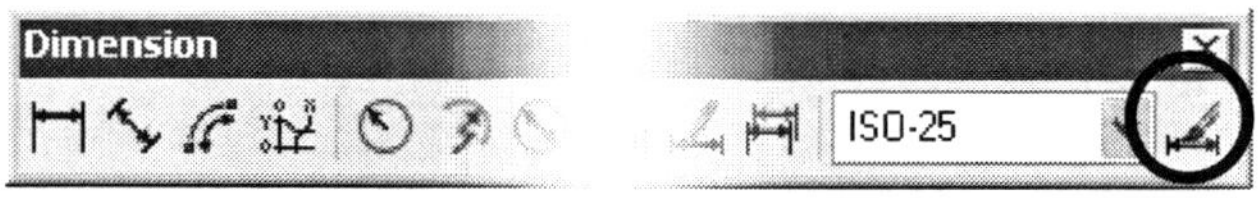

A dialog box will appear

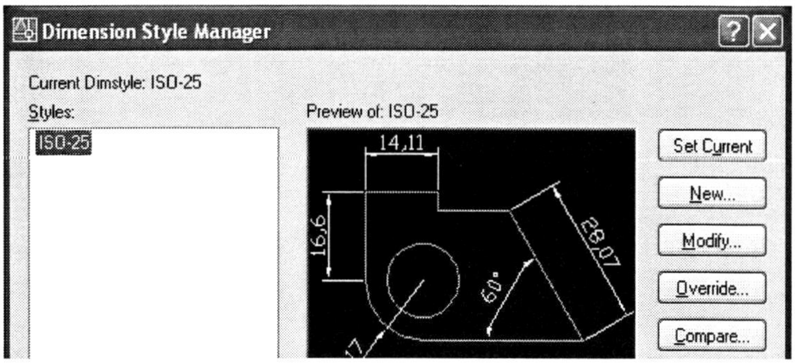

- Click 

A new dialog box will shows up

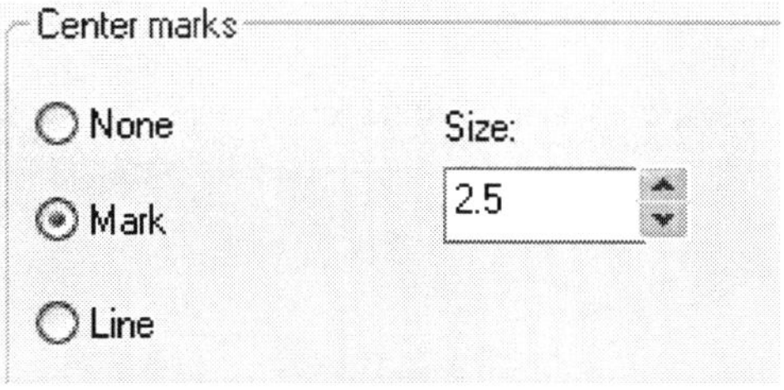

- Mark **Line**
- Key in the size 1
- Click **OK**
- Click **Close**

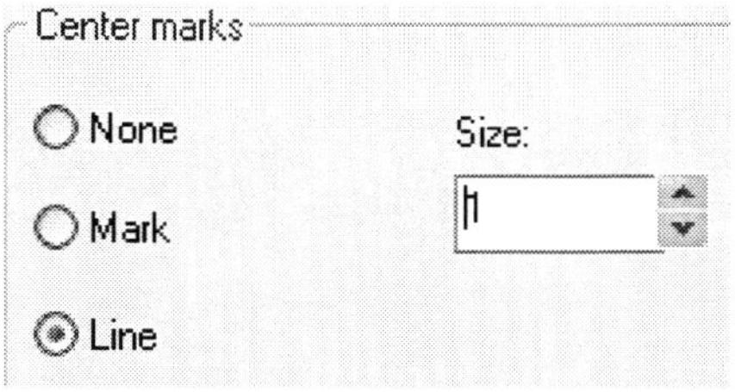

- Change layer to Midline
- Choose DIMCENTER - DCE 
- Pick the two circles ENTER

The centrelines are drawn in the circles

The result should look like this:

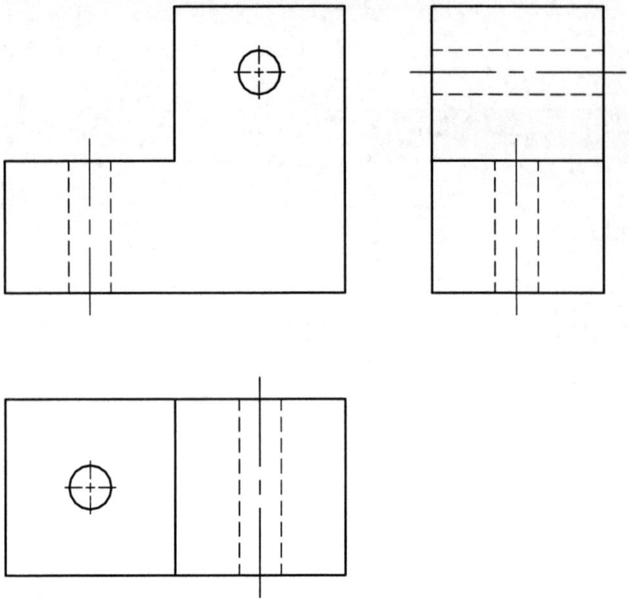

- Save the drawing

Fillet

Now we are going to make fillet in the view FRONT – the result should be as shown I the drawing below:

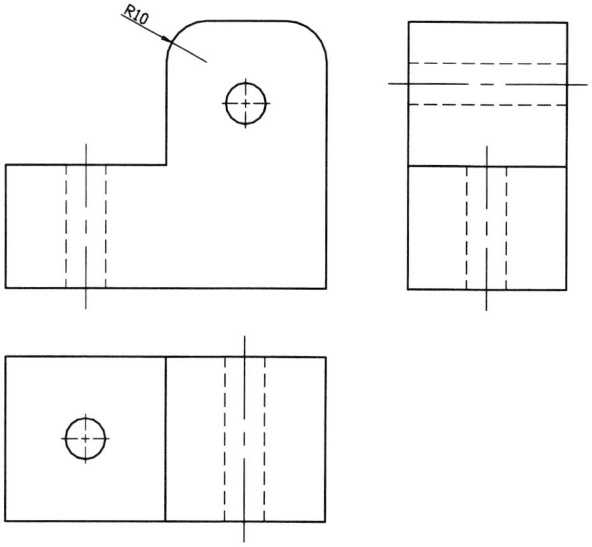

Exercise 07 - FILLET

- Choose FILLET 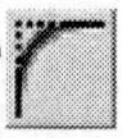
- Choose subcommand R ENTER
- Key in 10 (Radius) ENTER
- Hit ENTER to reuse the FILLET command
- Pick the line at point 1
- Pick the line at point 2

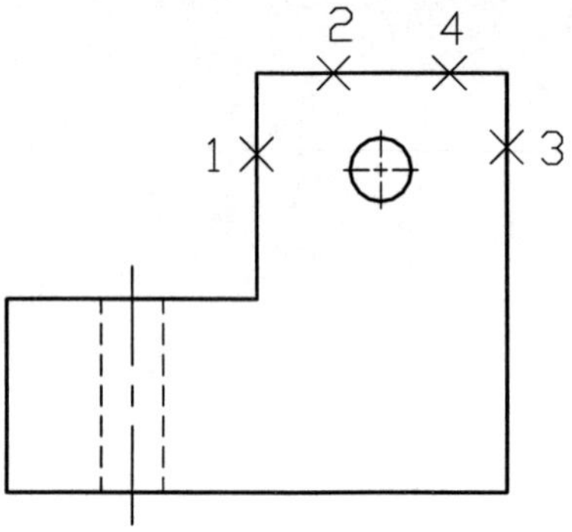

- Repeat the FILLET command by hitting ENTER
- Pick the line at point 3
- Pick the line at point 4

The result should be as shown:

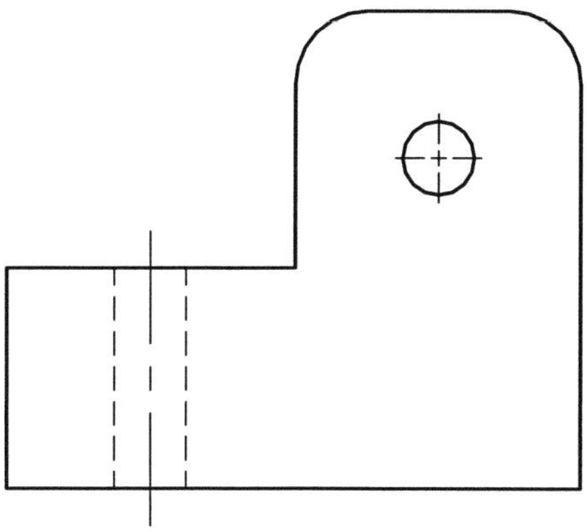

- Save the drawing

Chamfer

Now we are going to CHAMFER the left corner in view FRONT

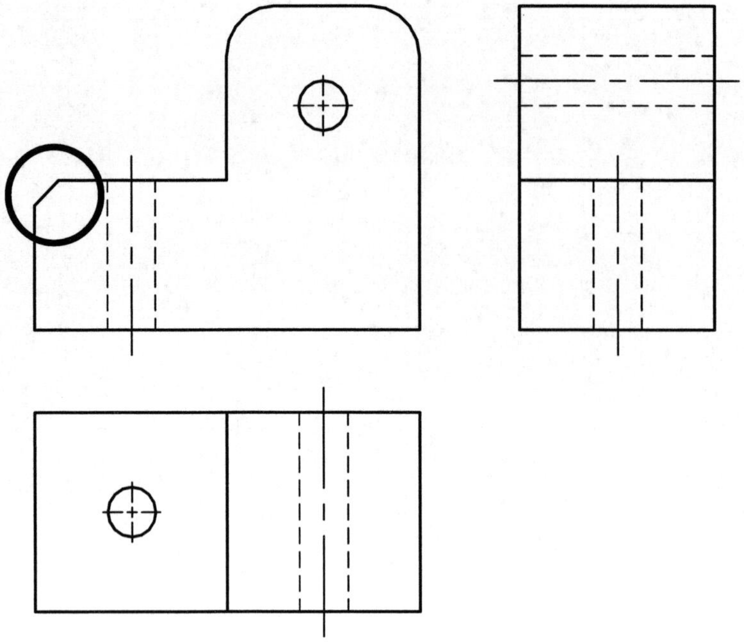

Exercise 08 - CHAMFER

Choose CHAMFER

Choose the subcommand D (ENTER)

Key in 5 (Distance 1) (ENTER)

Hit ENTER (Distance 2)

Hit ENTER

Pick the line at point 1

Pick the line at point 2

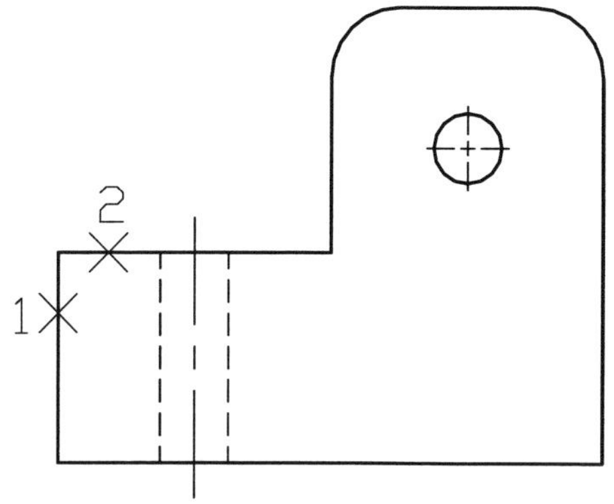

Save the drawing

Line type scale

The layers HIDDEN LINE and MIDLINE are defined with the line type hidden and dash dot. Sometimes you are not able to see the lines as you wish. The spaces could be too small or too big.

This problem is solved using the command LTSCALE.

Your drawing could look like this:

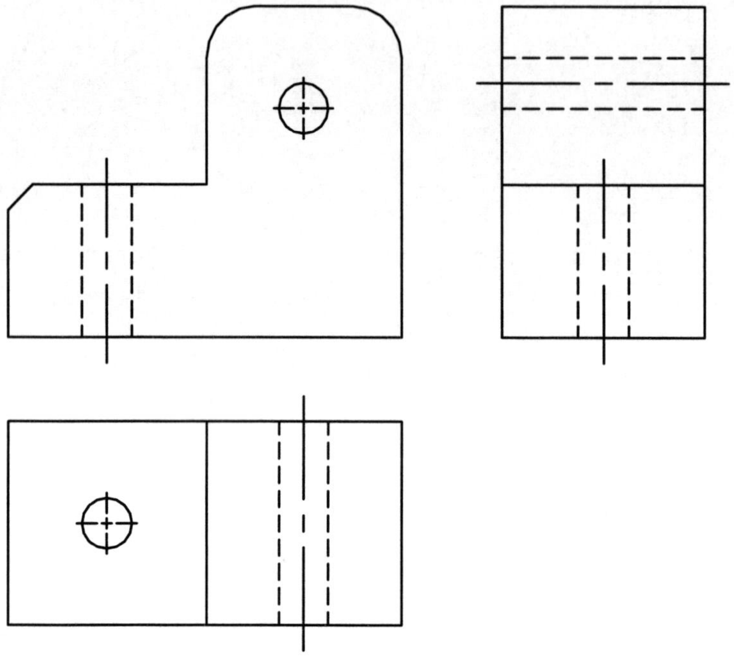

Exercise 09 - LTSCALE

Key in the command LTSCALE – just type LTS

Give LTSCALE the value 0.25

The spaces in the lines will appear shorter on the screen.

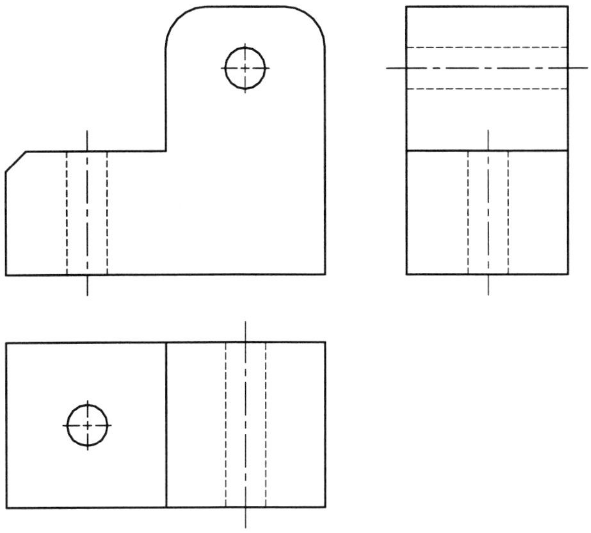

Try some different values of LTSCALE.

Offset

We are going to offset the two lines which show the chamfer. They are in the views TOP and LEFT. – look at the drawing below:

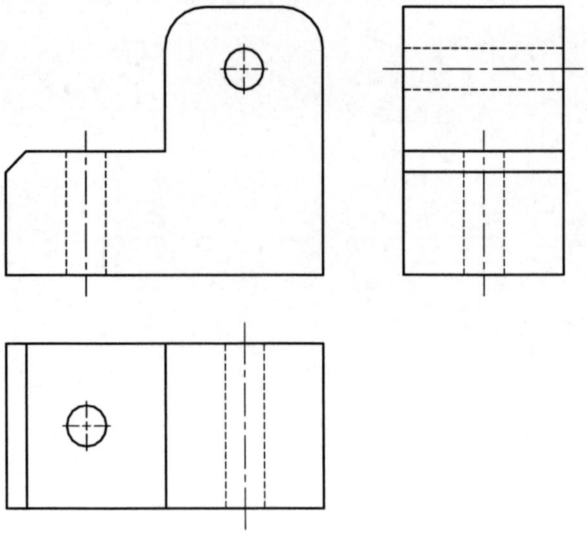

Exercise 10 --OFFSET

- Choose **OFFSET** – just type **O** or click this button

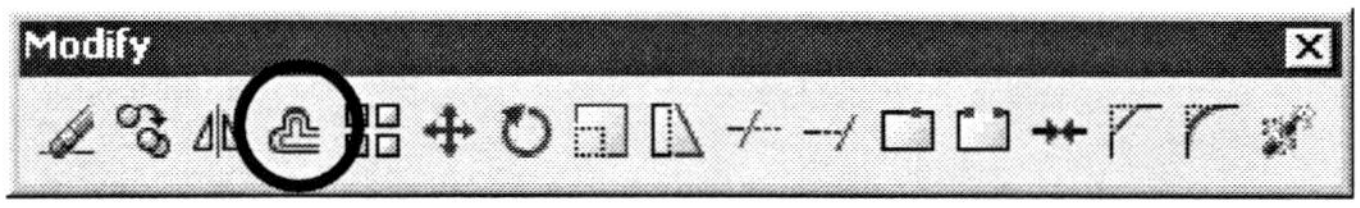

- Key in the distance 5
- Click the line at point 1
- Click at point 2
- Click the line at point 3
- Click at point 4

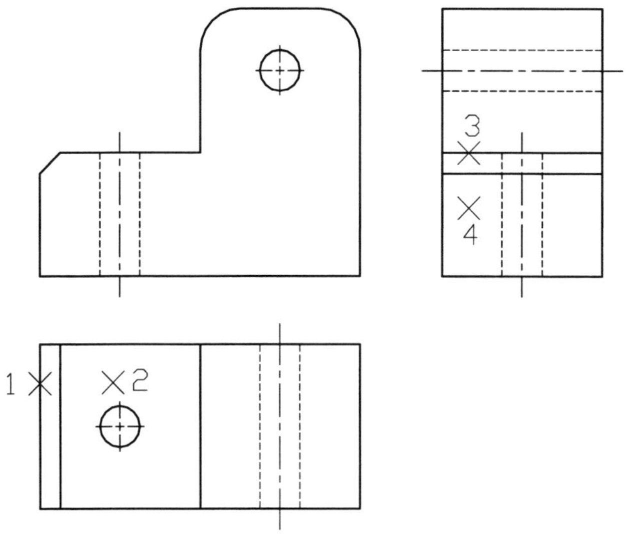

- Save the drawing

ZOOM

We are now going to look at a detail in the drawing and at that reason we will zoom a part of the drawing.

Exercise 11 - ZOOM

- Use the wheel on the mouse zooming this part of the drawing.

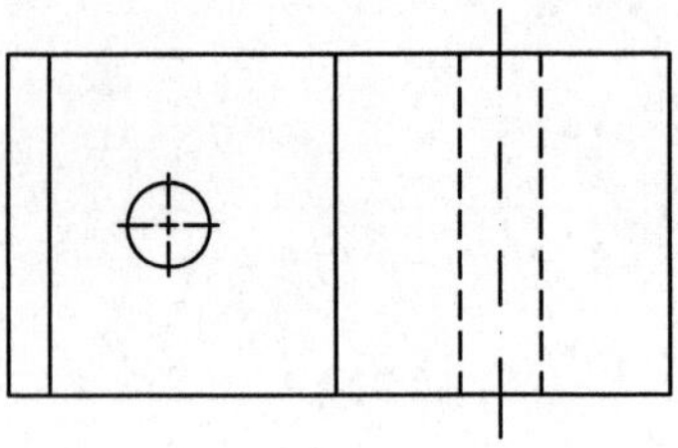

Trim

Some of the lines need a trim. We want the drawing look like this:

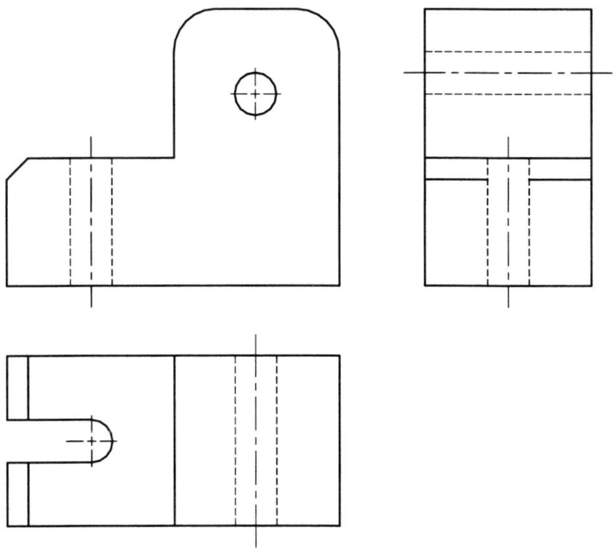

Exercise 12 - TRIM

- Draw the missing lines as shown in the drawing below:

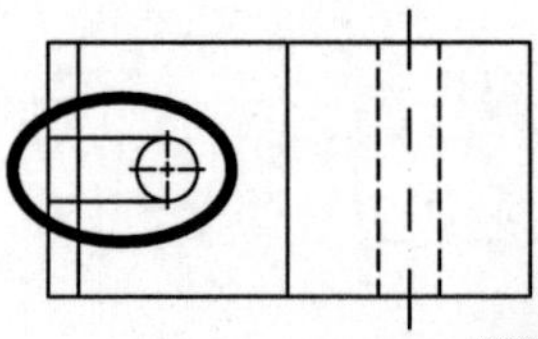

- Choose **TRIM**

When you are asked about

Select objects

You just hit ENTER – then all objects are selected

- Pick the elements that you want to remove from the drawing.

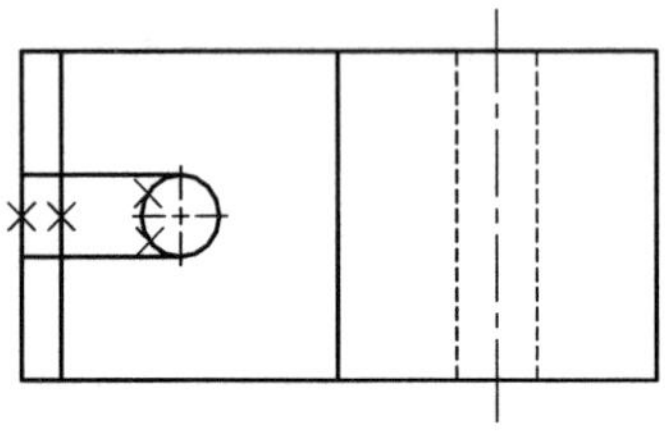

- Use the same method trimming lines in the view LEFT.

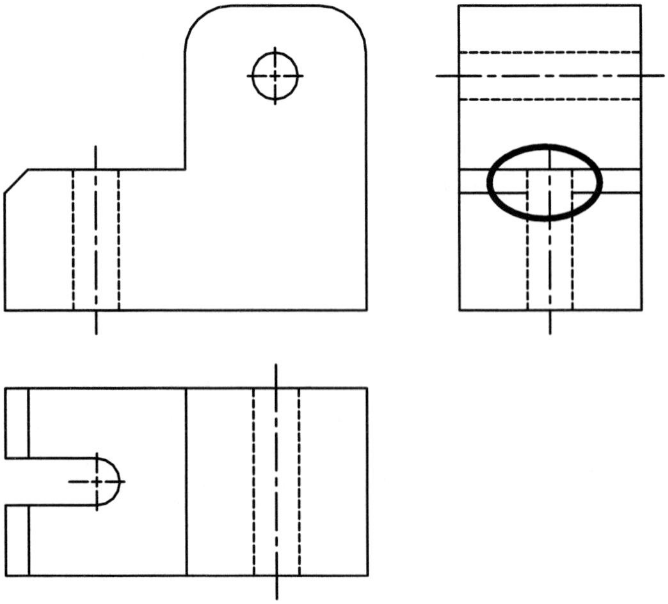

Exercise 13 - ERASE

Now we are going to erase a line which is no longer needed.

- Zoom the view FRONT

  Choose **ERASE** 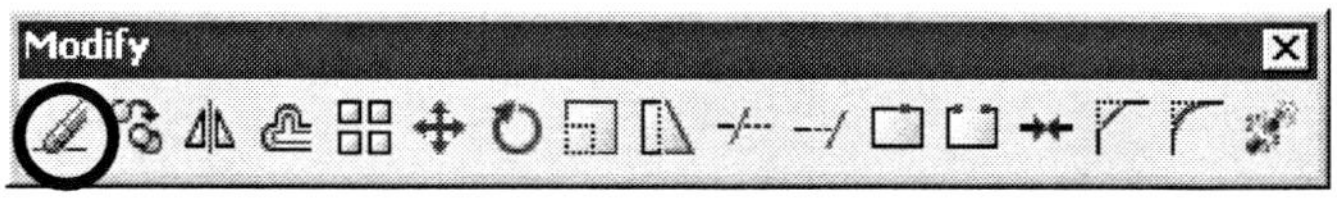

- Pick the left hidden line ENTER

The drawing should look like this:

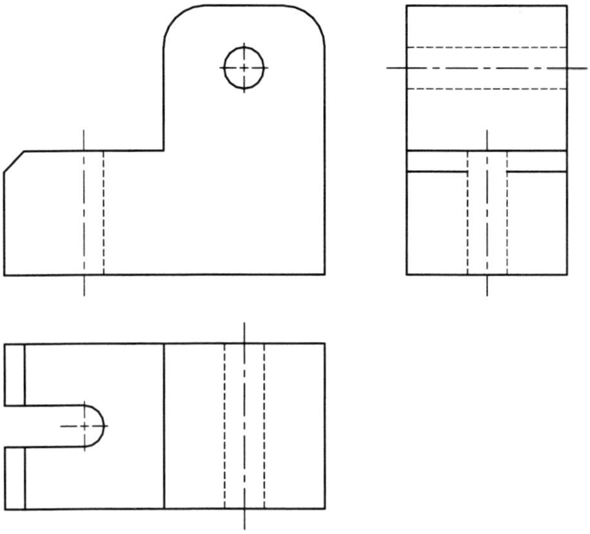

- Save the drawing

Exercise 14 – Change layer

- Pick the two hidden lines in the view LEFT

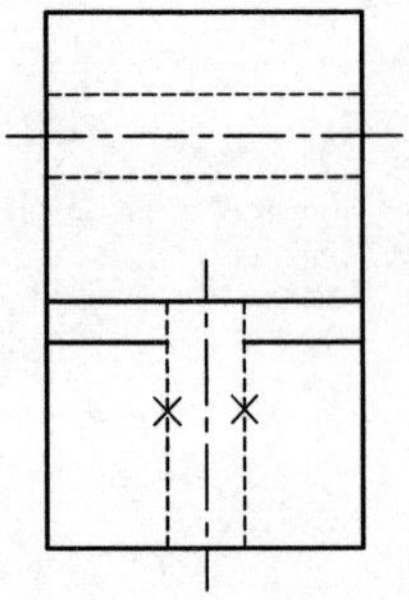

- In the layer drop down choose the layer FRAME

The two lines are change to be continuous

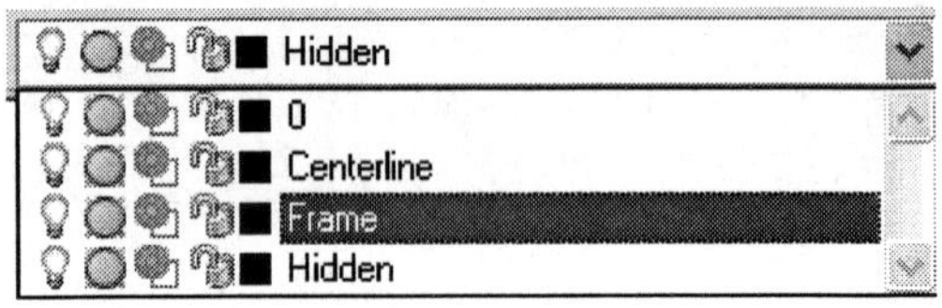

This part of the drawing is finished – Dimensions are made later.

- Save the drawing

Section view

Now we are going to make a section view in the drawing. We need to make this manually as there is no function for that in AutoCAD.

We will make the section line as a WBLOCK, so it can be used in other drawings. A section view is named with letters and we will make some attributes for those letters.

When we have finished the section view it should look like this:

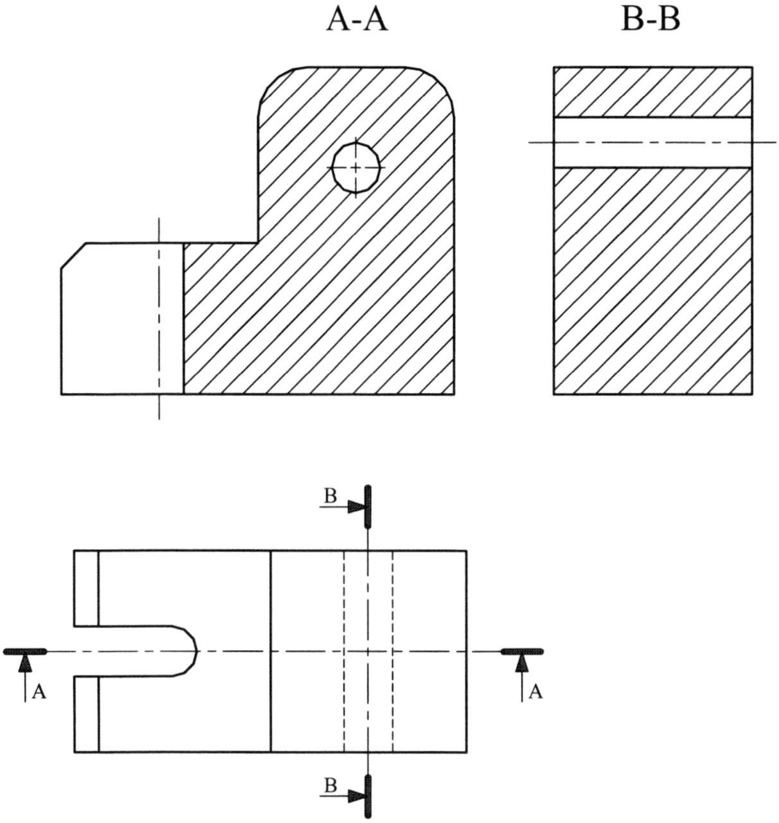

Exercise 15 – Polyline

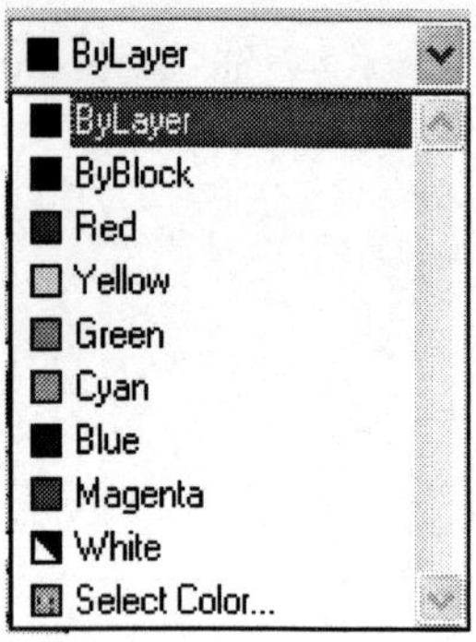

- Change the layer to SECTION
- Draw a horizontal line 7.5 mm – you can draw the line where you wish on the screen.
- Mark the line and change its color to yellow pulling down the color menu:
- Choose **PLINE** 
- Choose **OSNAP MID** 
- Choose the subcommand Width – just key in W
- Choose the start width 0 (zero)
- Choose the end width 2
- Move the cursor vertical down on the screen and key in 4
- Choose again the subcommand Width
- Choose the start width 0 (zero)
- Key in the end width 0
- Move the cursor vertical down on the screen and key in 6

Now the little drawing should look like this:

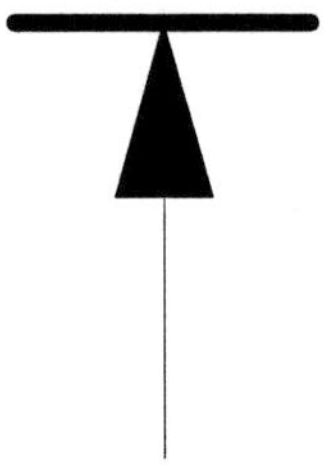

Attributter

The Start and the end of the section line has to be named with a letter and we will do that by making an attribute. If you reuse the section arrow more than once – you can change the name of the section.

Exercise 16 - Attributes

- Choose **DDATTDEF** at the keyboard - **ATT**

A dialog box will appear

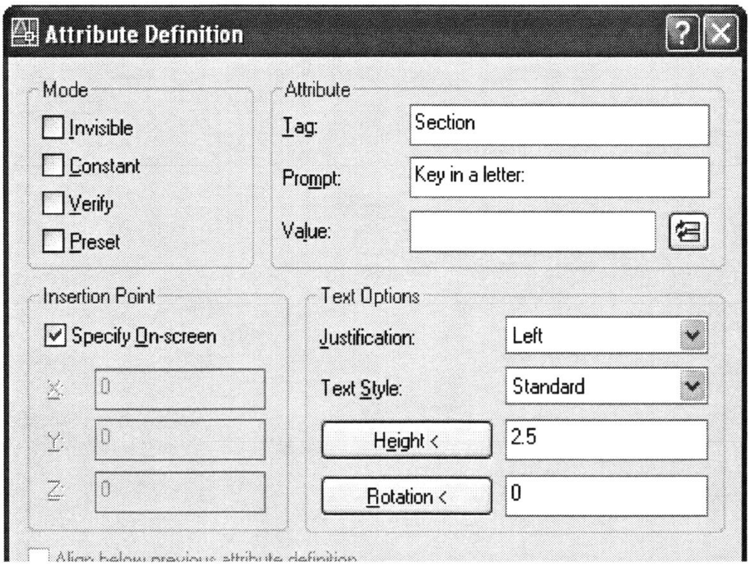

- In the area **Tag** type in the name **ESCTION**
- In the area **Prompt** – type in the words: **Key in a letter**
- Key in 2.5 in the area **Height**
- Click OK
- and pick the insertion place for the attribute – look at the image below:

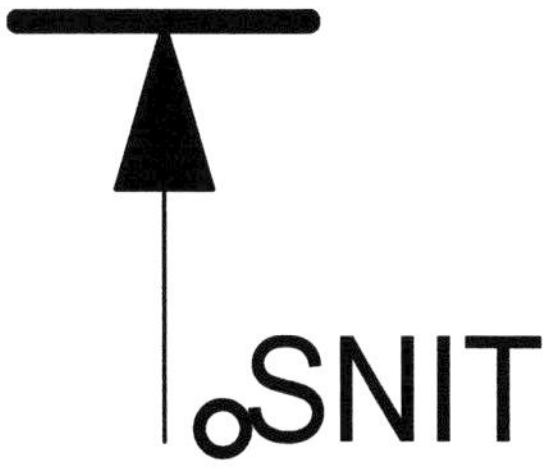

- The attribute shall be placed 2 mm to the right of the endpoint of the arrow.

- Click OK and place the attribute TAG 2 mm to the right of the endpoint of the vertical line.

The word **SECTION** is now placed as shown.

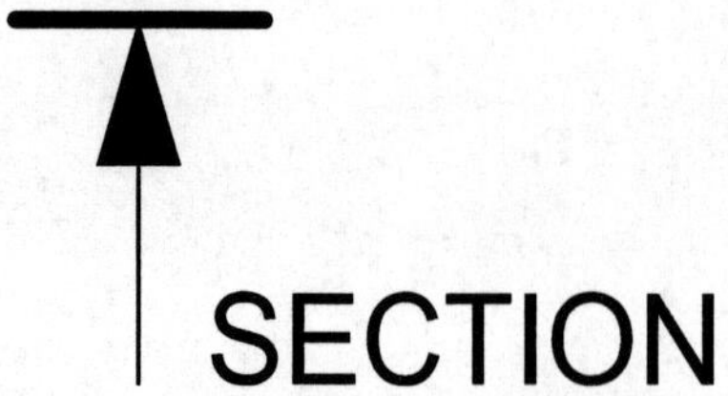

WBLOCK

We are now going to make a **WBLOCK** of the section arrow.

- Choose **WBLOCK** by typing **W**

A dialog box shows up

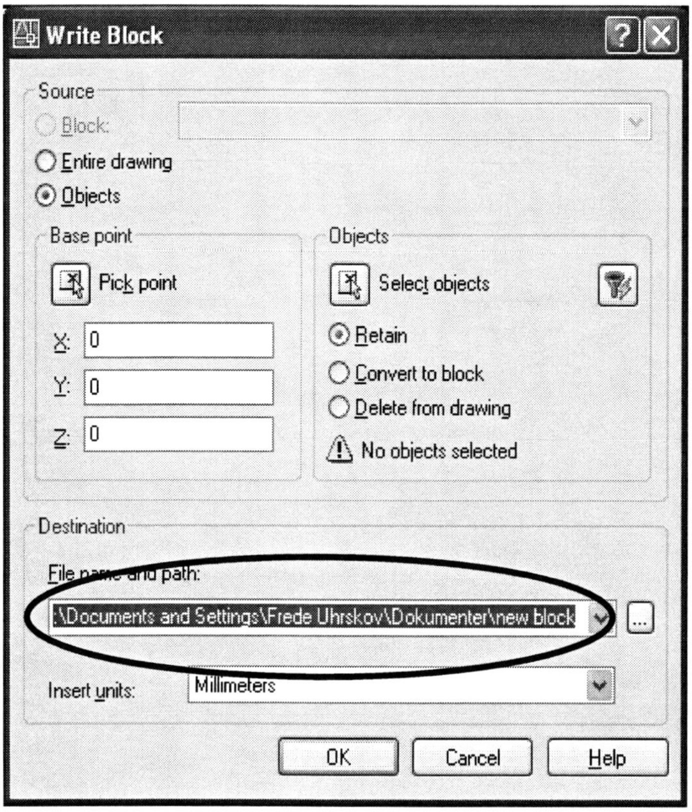

- In the field **File name and path** the name of the block – in this case the name is **START**

- Choose **Pick point** 

- And choose the right endpoint of the horizontal line as the insertion point of the block

- Choose Select objects 

  And choose the arrow, the line and the text

- Mark **Retain** 

- Choose **OK**

- Use the method making a WBLOCK with the insertion point in the left side of the line.

This new block could you call **END**

Now we have made 2 WBLOCKs which can be used in all other drawings.

Drawing the section line

Exercise 17 – Drawing the section line

- Zoom to the view TOP
- Erase the center marks in the drawing
- Change to the layer **Section line**
- Draw a line from the midpoint of the arc trough the drawing to the right

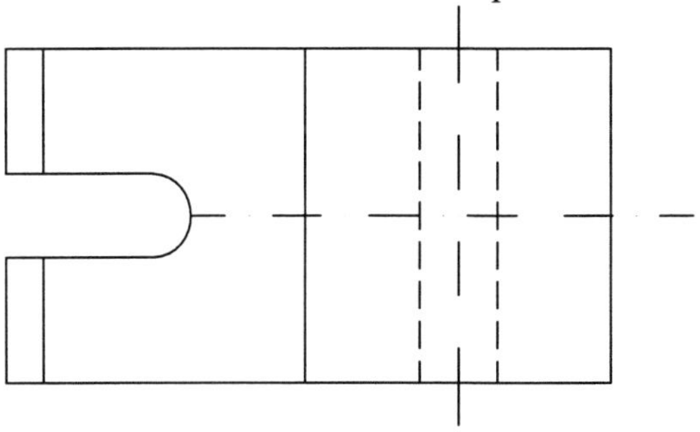

- Mark the line so you see the GRIPS
- Click the left grip and lengthen the line trough the drawing to the left

The drawing should look like this:

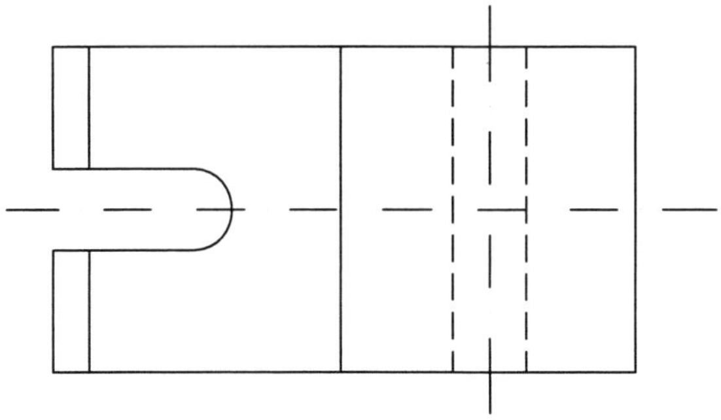

- Save the drawing

Insert

Now we are going to insert the START and the END wblocks in the drawing.

Exercise 18 - INSERT

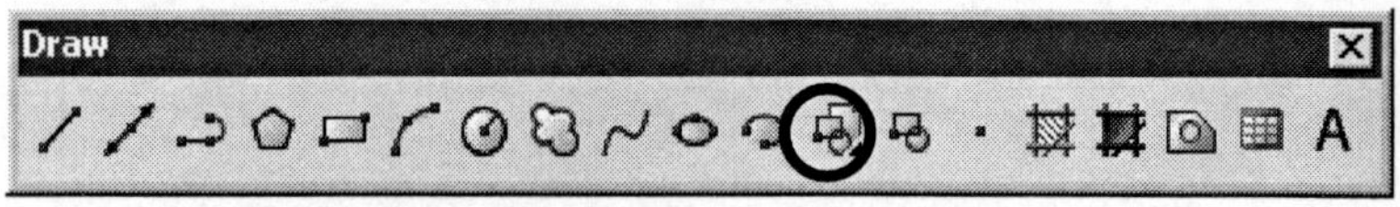

- Choose **INSERT**

A dialog box appears

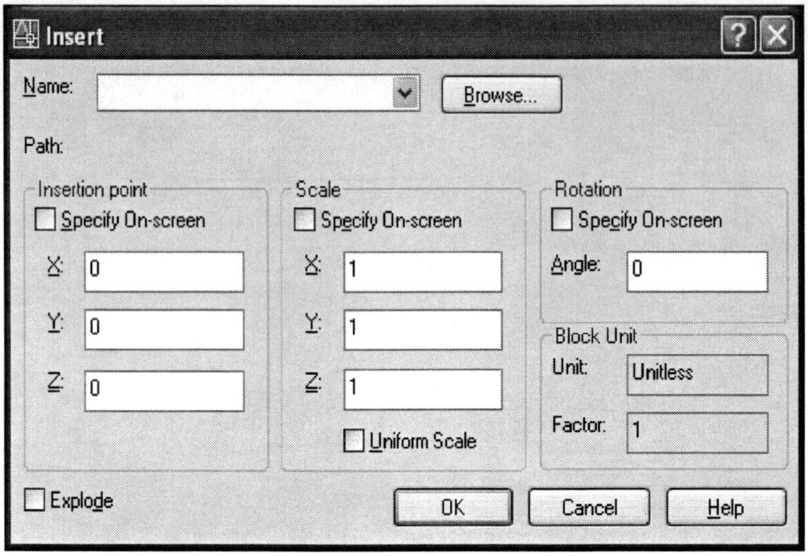

- Choose  and choose the Wblock you made earlier.

- Mark this field 

- Then you can place the block as you wish in the drawing.

- Click **OK**

- Place the block at the start of the section line – in the left side.

- Key in the letter **A** as the section name
- Repeat in the other end og the section line.

Your drawing should look like this.

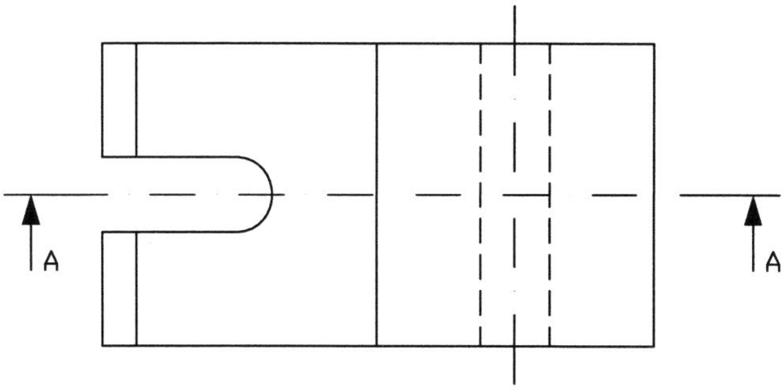

- Repeat the process with section **B** – be award of that the blocks shall be rotated when you make the insert.

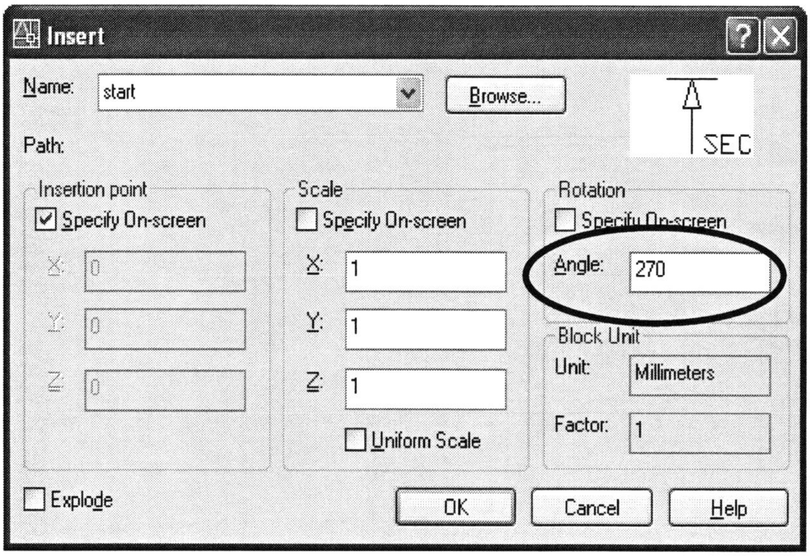

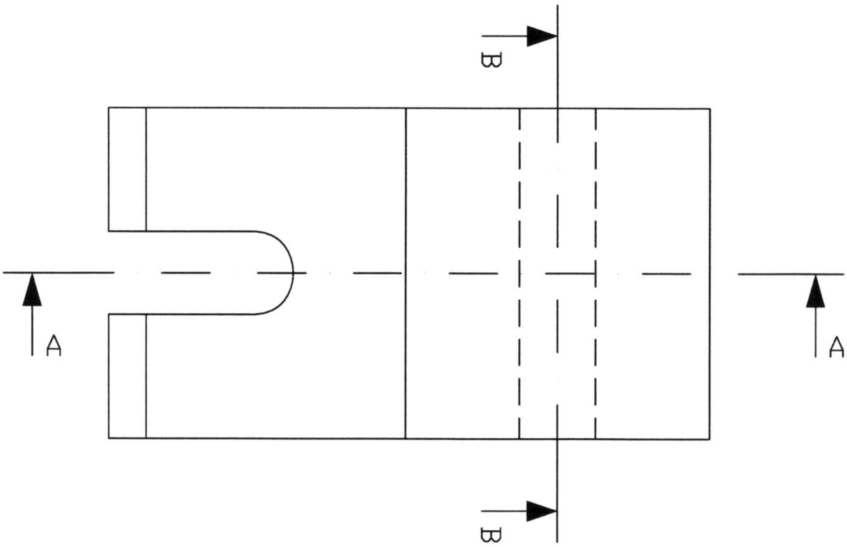

The section name B has to be rotated.

- Double click the section name B

A dialog box appears:

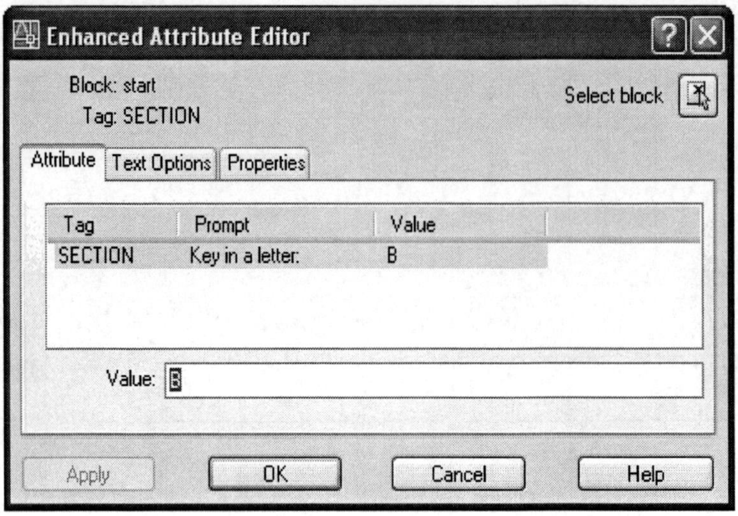

- Choose the tab **Text Options** 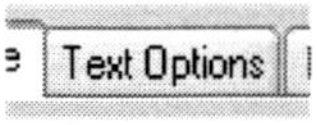

In this dialog box key in the value 0 in the field **Rotation** and choose **Top center** in the field **Justification** -look the picture below

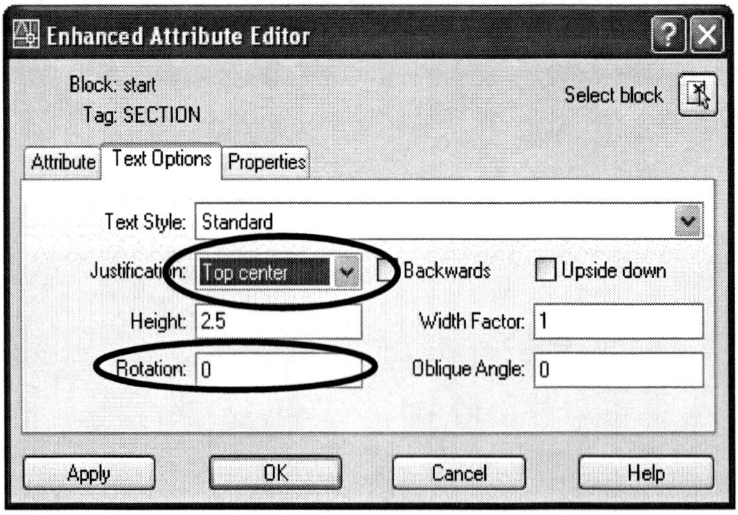

Use the same method rotating the other section letter.

Now the drawing should look like this:

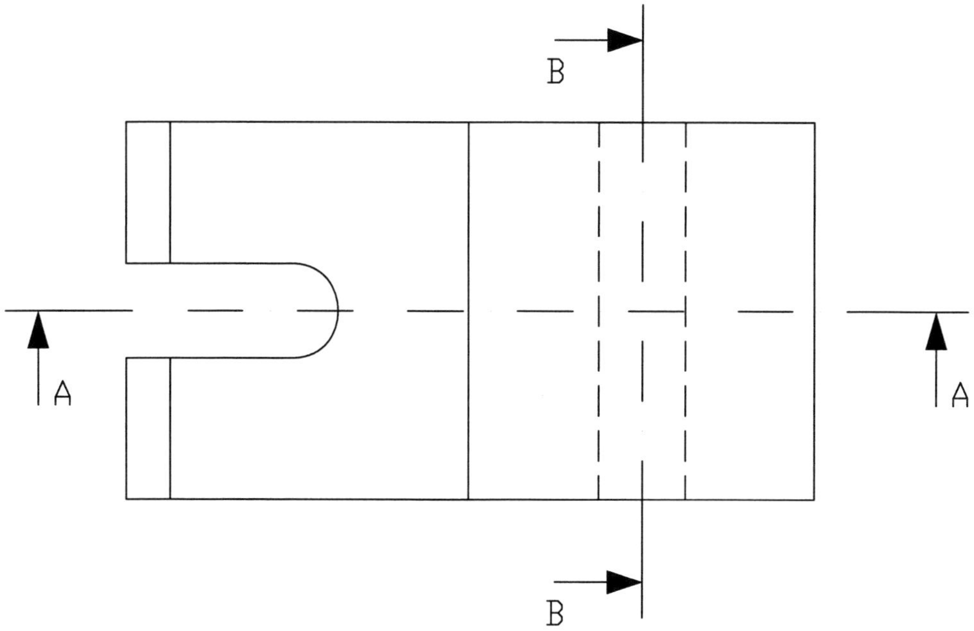

Hatching

Exercise 19 - BHATCH

- Change the layer and erase unnecessary lines in the view LEFT, so that the drawing will look like this:

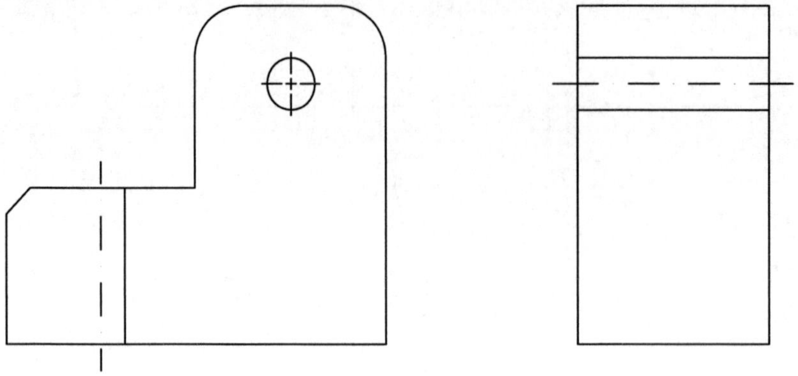

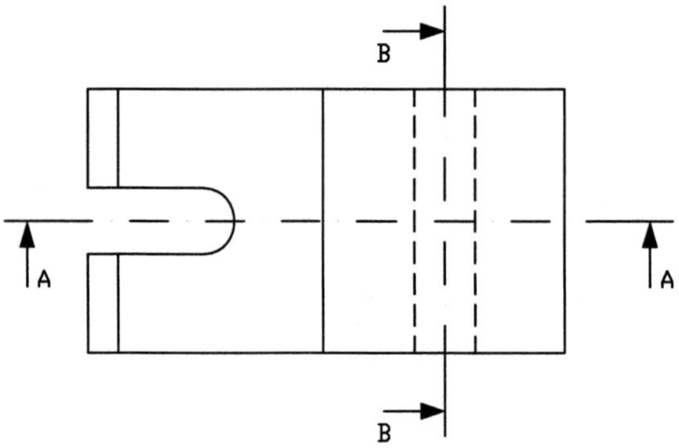

- Freeze the layer Centerline, then the hatching will be much easier.
- Change layer to Hatch
- Choose BHATCH 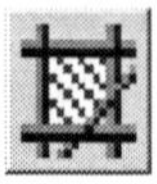

This dialog box will appear:

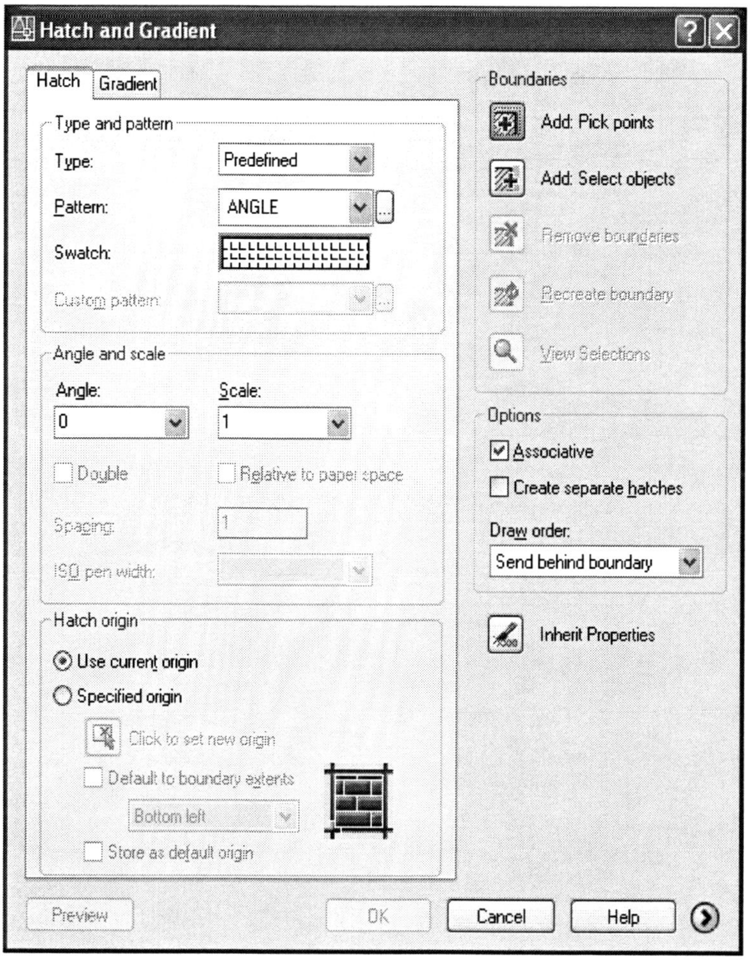

- Click the **Pattern** drop down

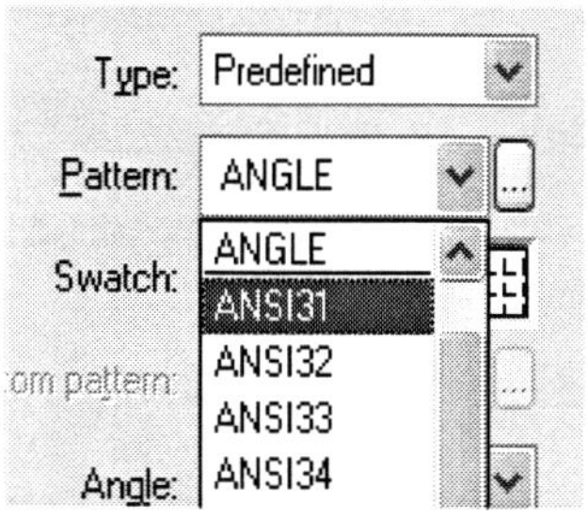

- Choose **ANSI31**
- Key in the value 3 in the field **Scale**
- Choose Add Pick points 

Mark the shown areas

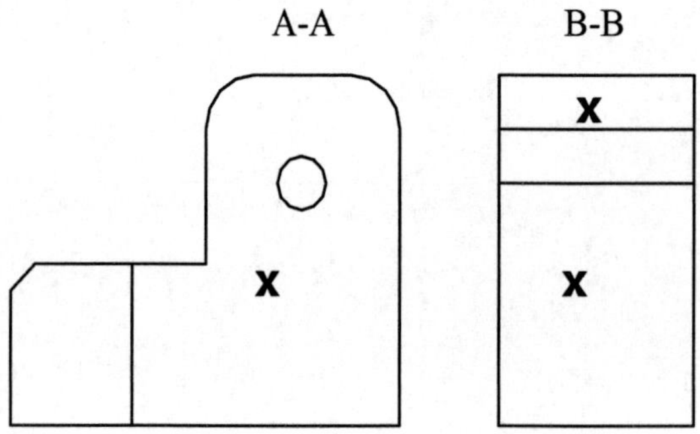

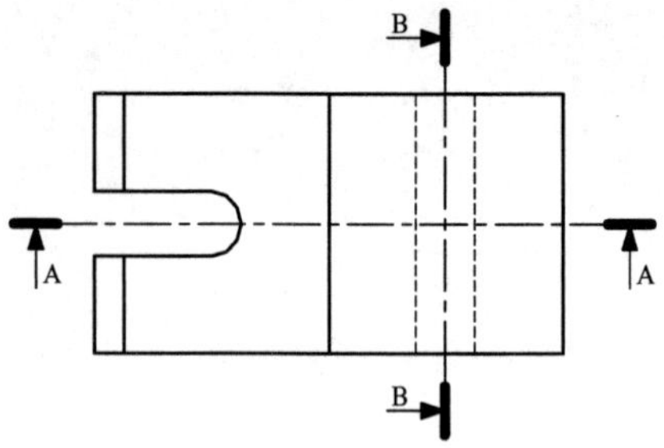

The areas are now marked

- Hit ENTER
- Choose **Preview**

A preview picture is shown

- If the hatch is as you wish – hit ENTER – if you want to change the parameters of the hatch – hit ESC
- Change the scale until you are satisfied
- Choose OK

Now the hatch is finished

- Thaw the frozen layer

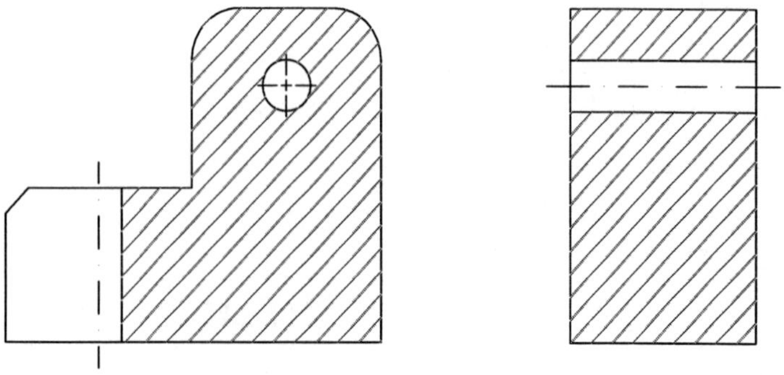

DTEXT

Exercise 20 - DTEXT

- Change the layer to **Text**
- Choose DTEXT 
- Point out the start point of the text **A-A**
- Key in the text high - 2.5
- Key in the rotation angle – 0
- Write the text
- Hit ENTER
- Move the cursor to the place on the screen where the text **B-B** is going to be placed an ckick the left button.
- Write the text
- Hit ENTER
- Hit ENTER

Notices that you have to hit ENTER twice to end the DTEXT command.

Your drawing should look like this:

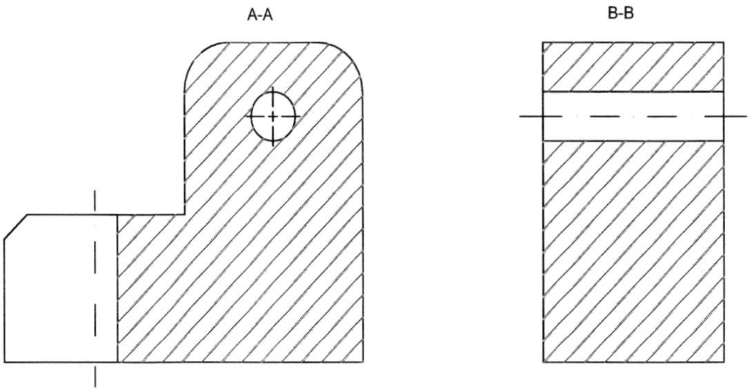

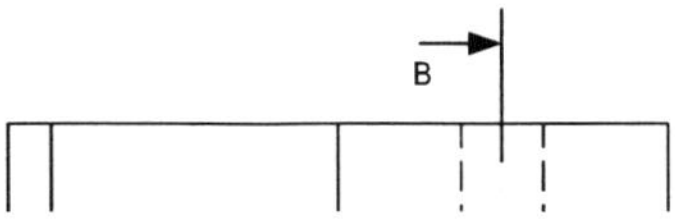

Dimension

Now we are going to dimension the block – not the section view.

The dimension is shown below:

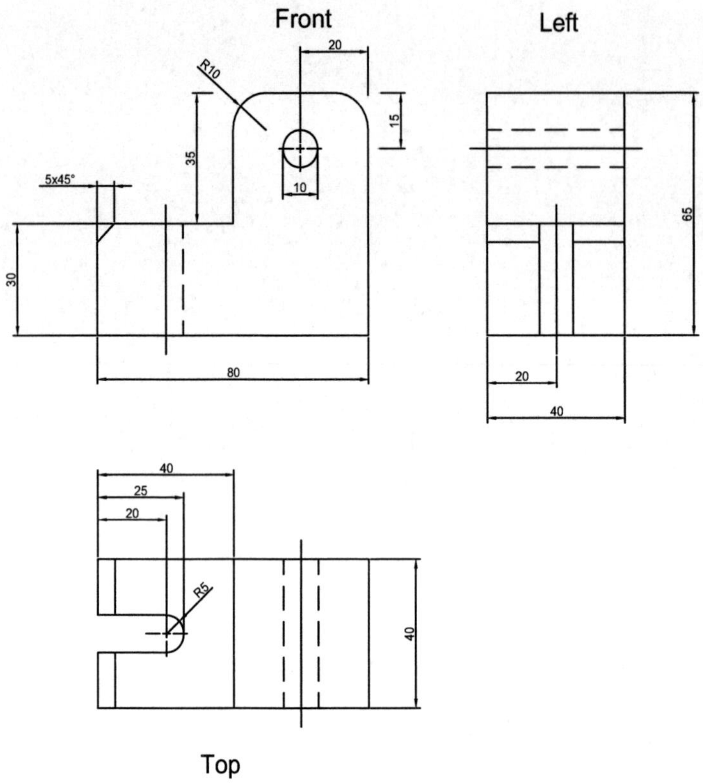

Exercise 21 - DIM

We will start with a little change of the dimension style.

- Choose the command DDIM 

The dimstyle dialog will appear

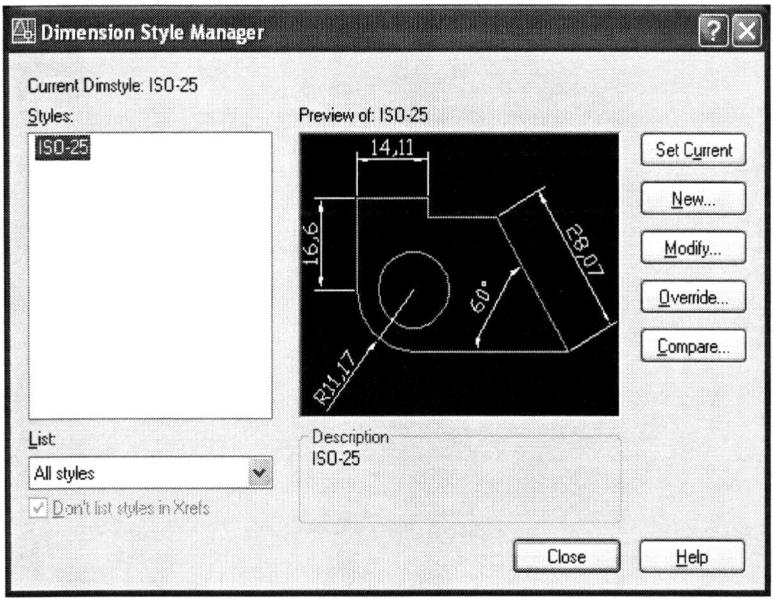

- Choose **Modify** 

- In the field **Offset from origin** key in the value 4
- Choose **OK**
- Choose **Close**

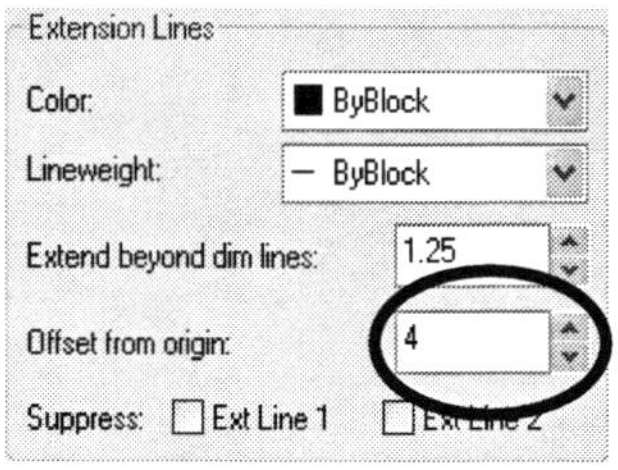

- Try to dimension the drawing as shown on the previous site.

Print/Plot

Exercise 22 - PLOT

In this section I will show none of the ways printing your drawing. I have chosen a method which uses layout.

Projection

Our first print will be of the projected drawing

This drawing is made in **Model**

Now we are going to print the drawing from **Layout**.

- Click the tab **Layout1** – now you are changing to paperspace, where you see a pice of paper and a window containing the drawing

First thing to do is defining the paper size.

- Wright click the tab **Layout1** and choose **Page Setup Manager**

The Page Setup Manager dialog box appears:

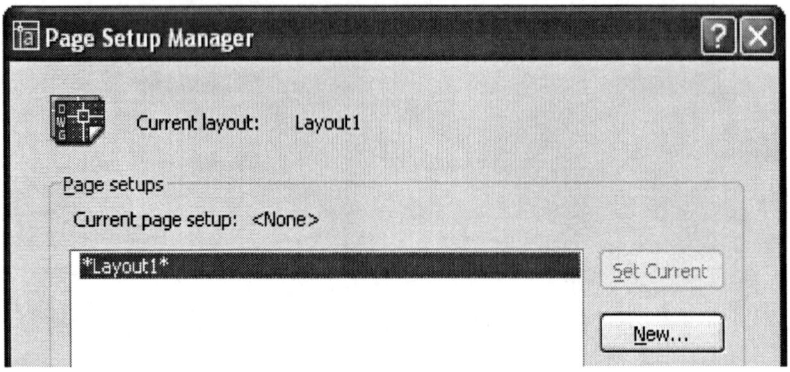

- Click **New**

Another dialog box appears:

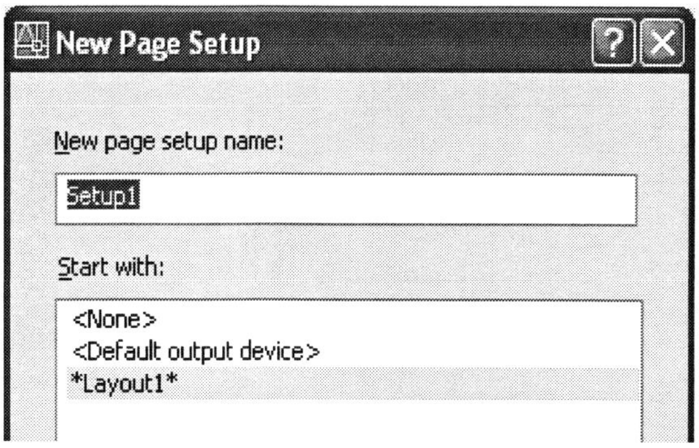

- Give the new layout a name in the field

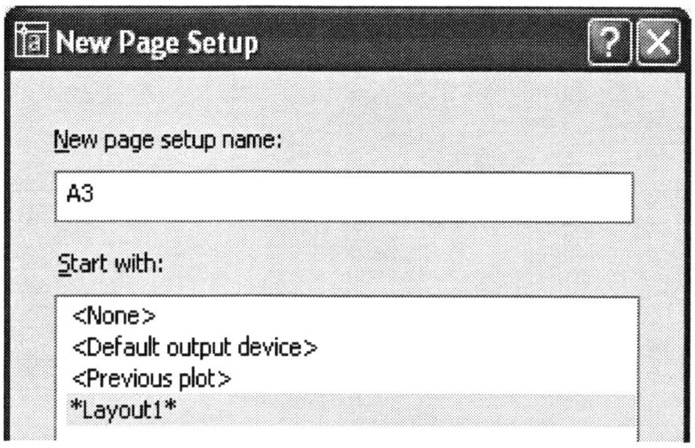

- Click **OK**

Now the **Page Setup** dialog box will appear.

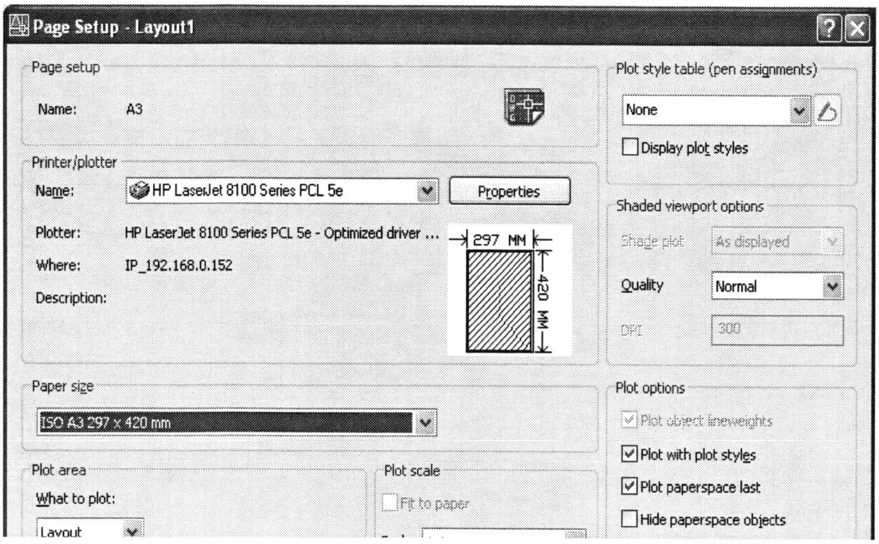

Start chose the printer, which you want to use.

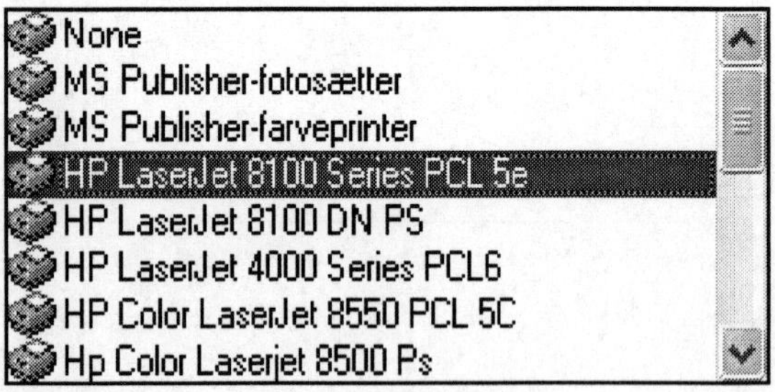

Choose the paper format that you want.

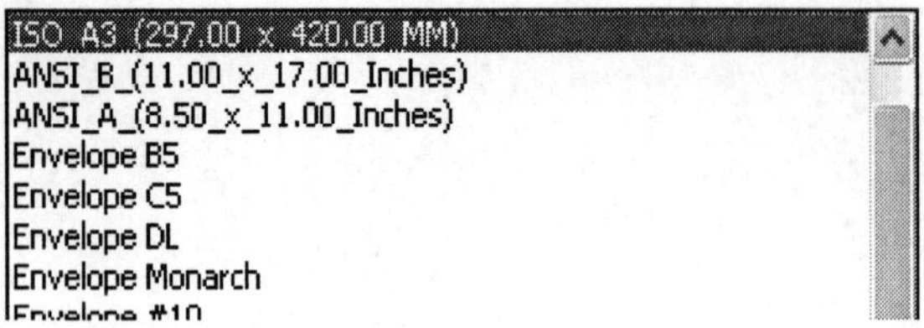

- Choose the colour table that you want - **Monochrome.ctb** is black/white print and **Acad.ctb** is colour print.

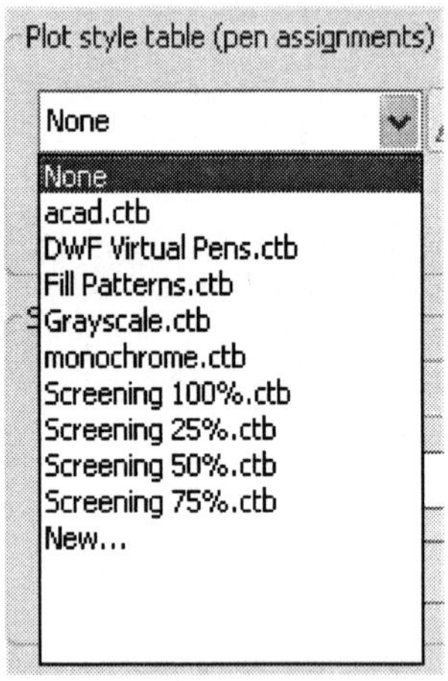

- Click OK

Back in **Page Setup** choose the name of the layout and click **Set current**

- Click **Close**

The chosen paper size (A3) is now shown in **Layout.** You see your drawing in a window in the middle of the paper.

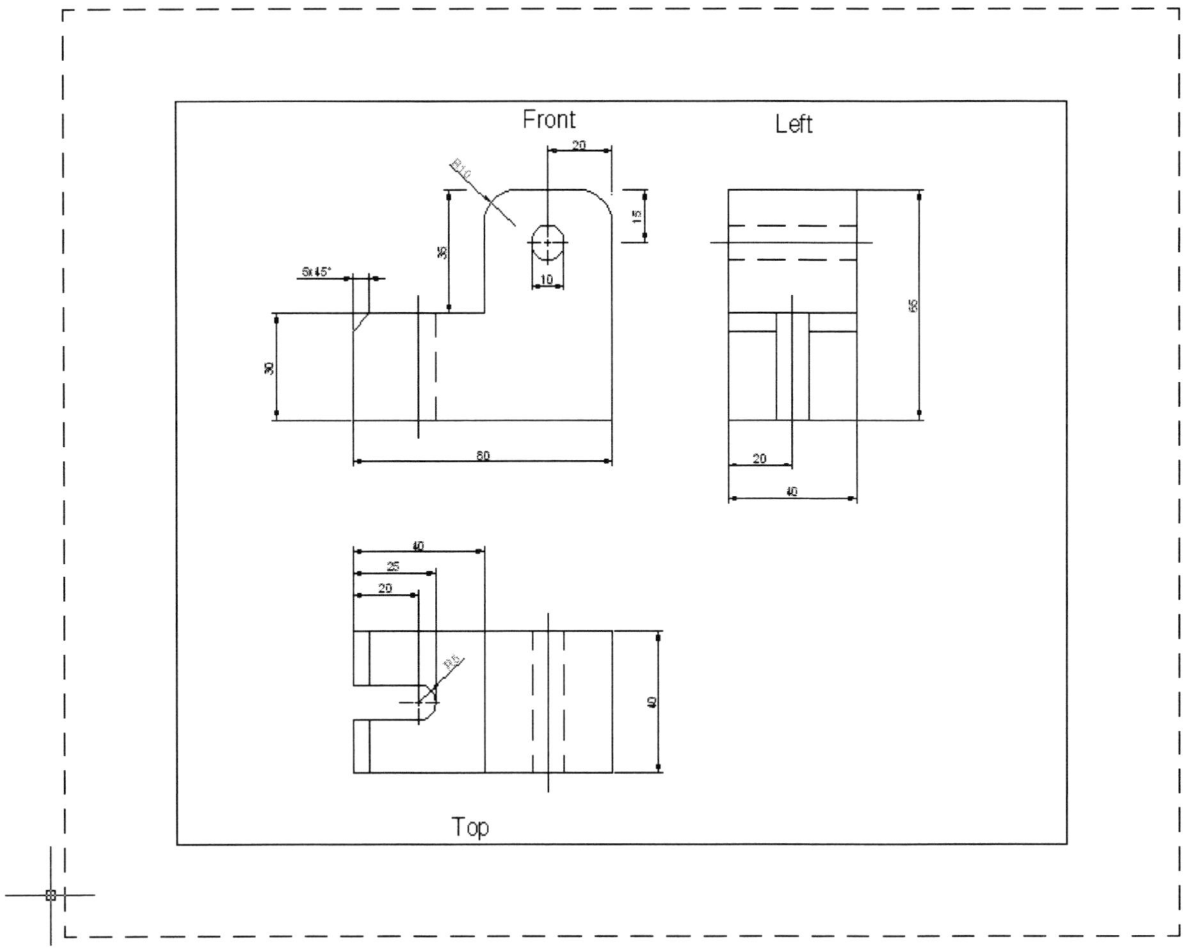

- Remove the window by clicking the frame and **Delete**

The drawing disappears – but we will find it again – just take it easy

- Key in the command **ATTDIA** on the command line and choose the value **1.**

- Insert an A3 title block – use one of your own or one from a firm

If the title block is made with attributes you will be asked what to write in the title block. You can change that later on, by double clicking at the title block.

The broken line is the maximum of the printer.

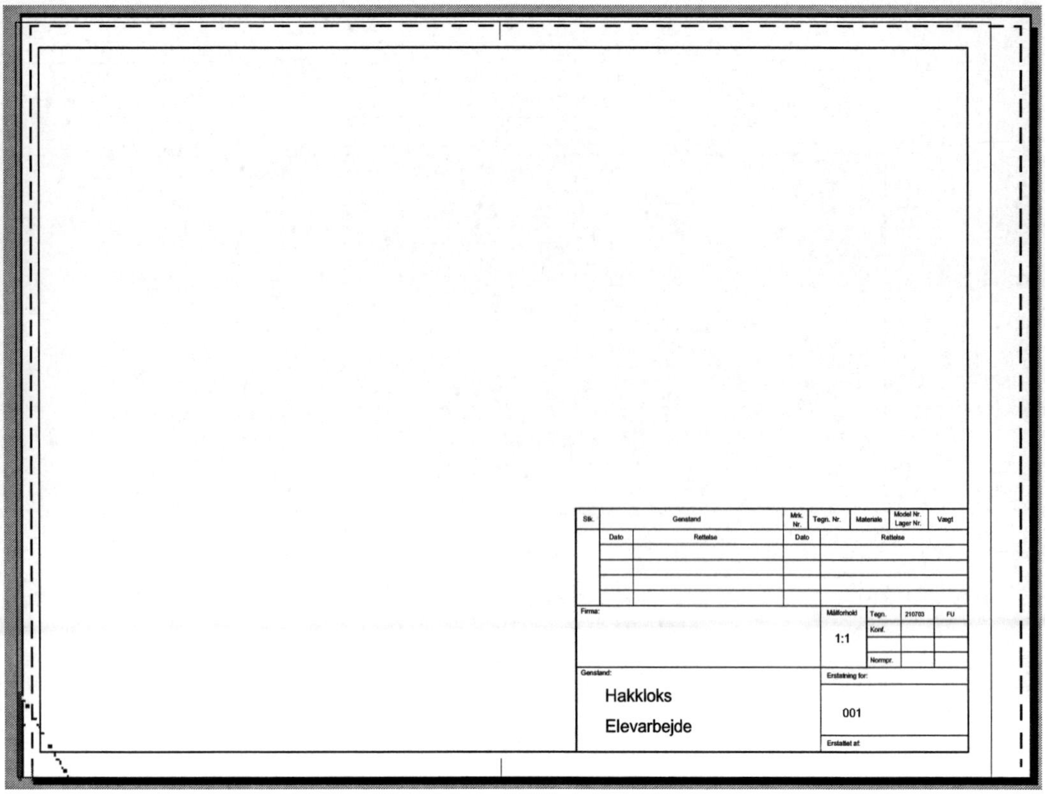

- Make a new layer **VPORTS** – make it black and click the printer, so that this layer not is going to be printed.

- Get the toolbar **Viewports** on the screen.

- Choose **Polygonal Viewport** 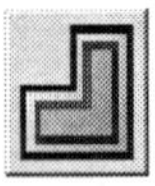 and draw a line along the inner lines of the title block.

When you finish your drawing, the original drawing appears in the window.

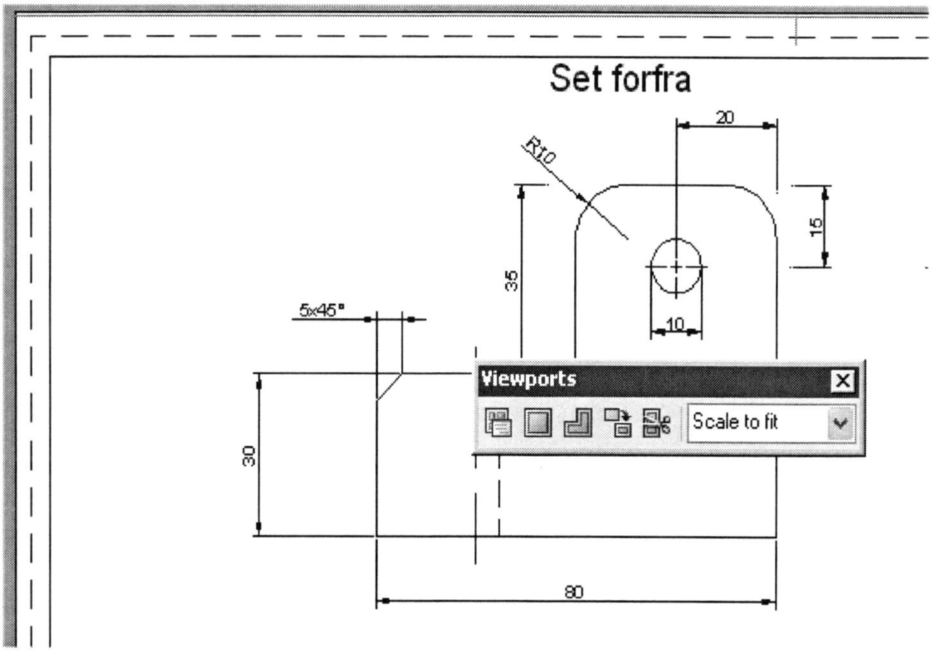

Now we just need to scale the drawing.

- Click the button 

The button change to show the name **Model** and the scale will be shown in the toolbar.

- Pull down and choose the scale 1:1.

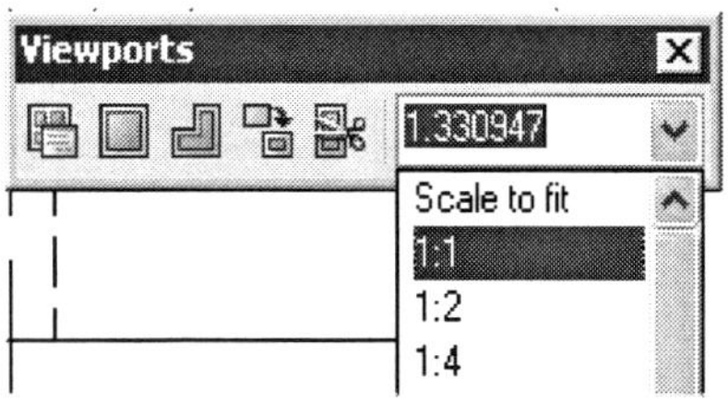

Notice that in AutoCAD 2007 this list can be user defined so that only the scale that you need is shown. You can do that from **Options -> User Preferences -> Edit Scale List**

Now the drawing will be scaled to 1:1 and it will be at its right place on the paper.

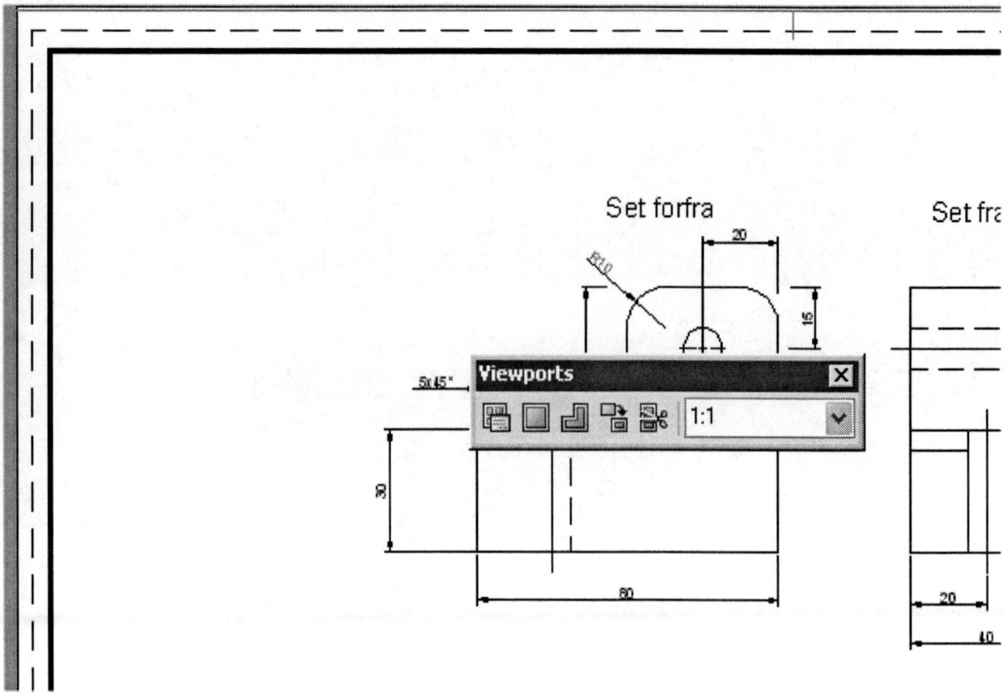

- Change back to **Layout** by clicking the button MODEL

Now we are ready printing the drawing.

- Click the printer button  or key in **Ctrl+P**.
- Click **OK** in the plotter dialog box.
- Save the drawing.

New Layout

Now we are going to make a new layout to the section view,

- Wright click **Layout2** and choose **Rename**.

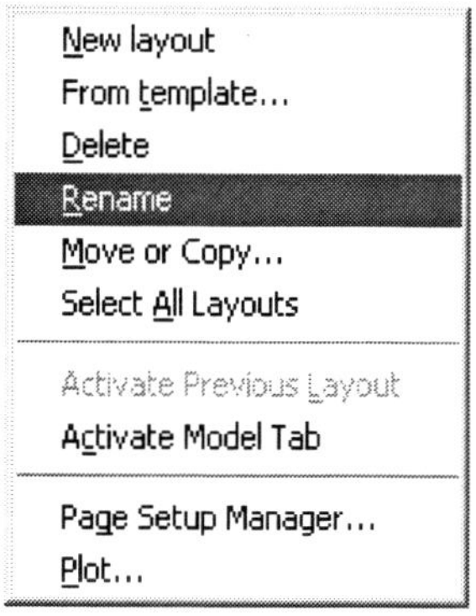

A dialog box appears, where you can change the name

- Click **OK**

The tab is now renamed 

- Click the **Model** tab, so you are on the black screen. Insert the section view drawing

You need to have both the section view and the projection drawing on the screen.

- Click the tab **Section view**

- Insert a title block on the paper and make a window on the paper in the same way as we did before.

- PAN the drawing until you see the section view in the window.

- Choose the scale 1:1

- Click the **Model button** 

- Print the drawing.

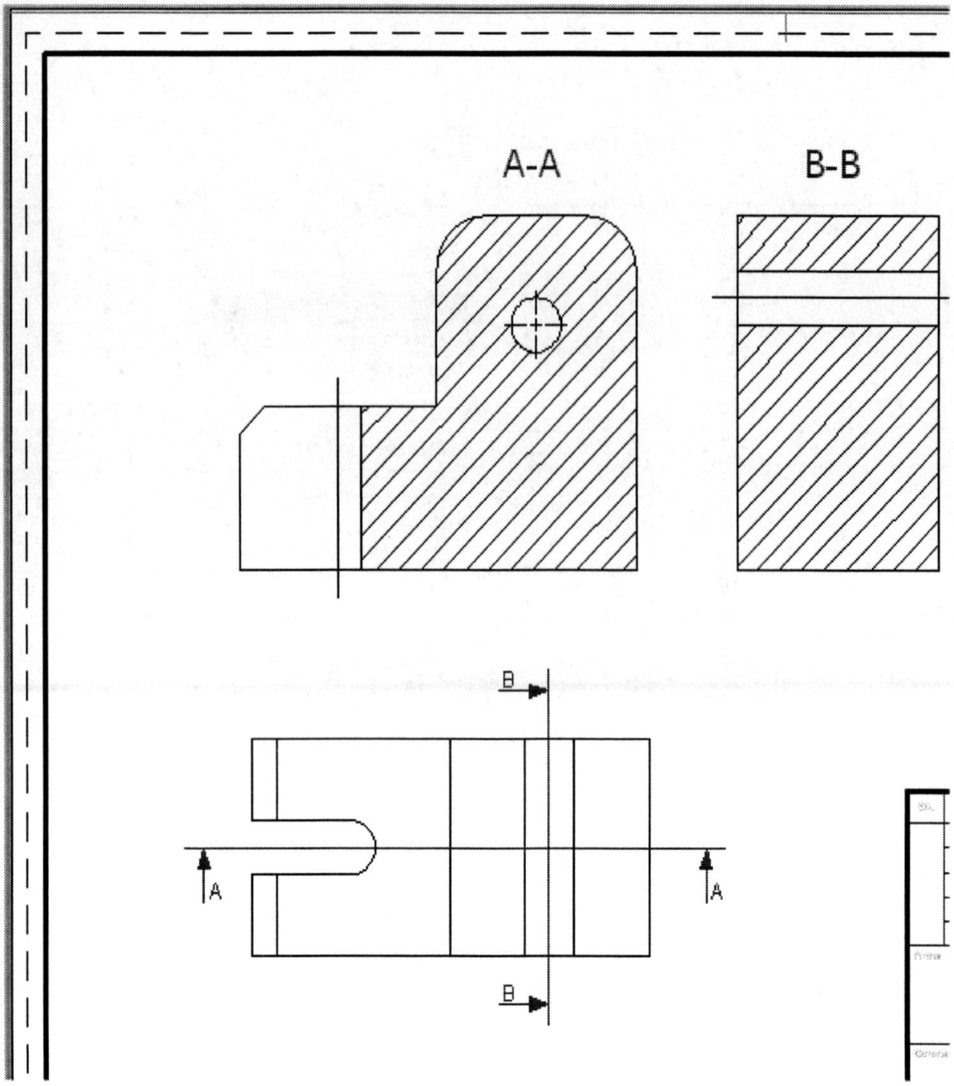
A-A
B-B
B
A
A
B

Exercises

on

Your own

The exercises on the next pages are meant as training the same commands as we has been using drawing the iron block.

Rocking link

We are going to draw a rocking link as you see in the drawings below.

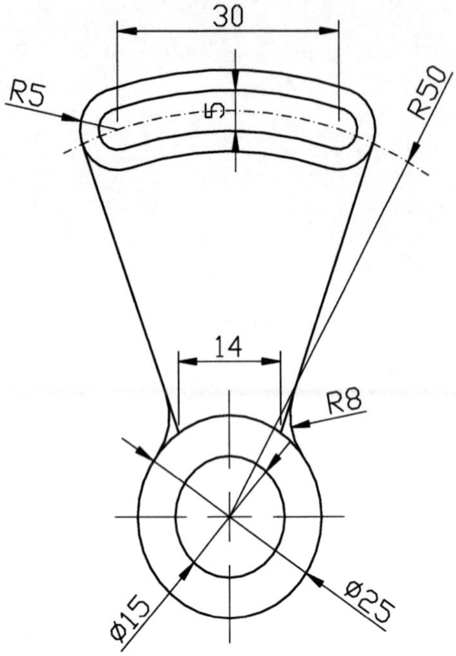

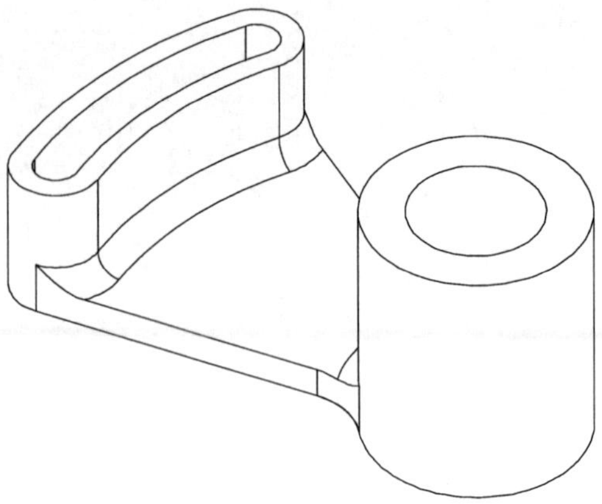

The rocking link is shown also in 3D, but this is not a part of the exercises – just to show you haw it really looks.

- Draw two concentric circles with the radiuses 7.5 and 12.5.

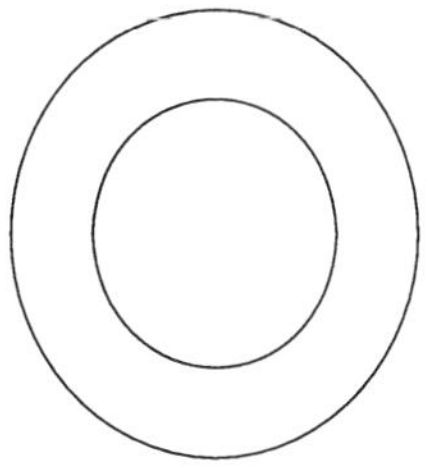

- Draw a construction line (XLINE) vertical trough the centre of the circles.

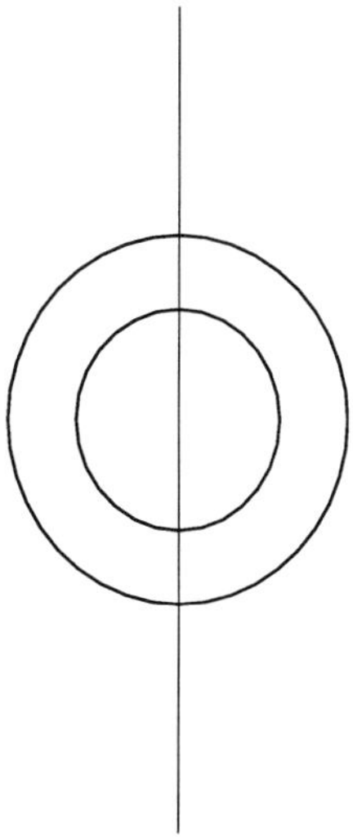

- Offset the construction line 15 mm. to both sides.

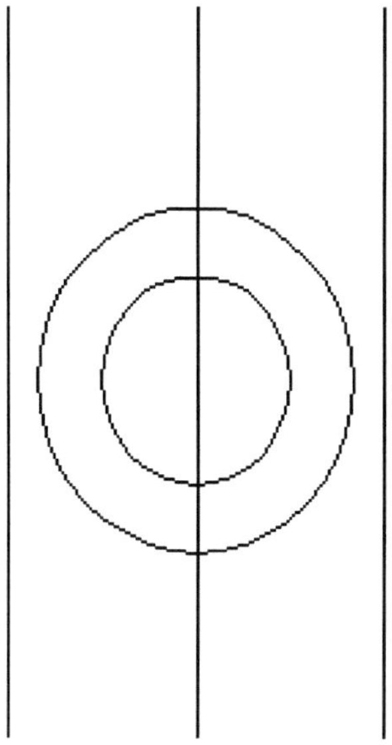

- Draw a circle with radius 50 and with the same centre as the other circles. Draw this circle on a layer using DAS-DOT line type.

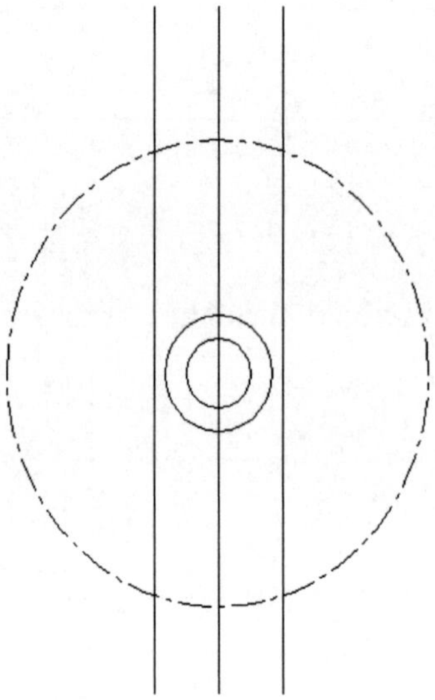

- In the intersection between the big circle and the two outer vertical lines draw two concentric circles with the radiuses 2.5 and 5.0.

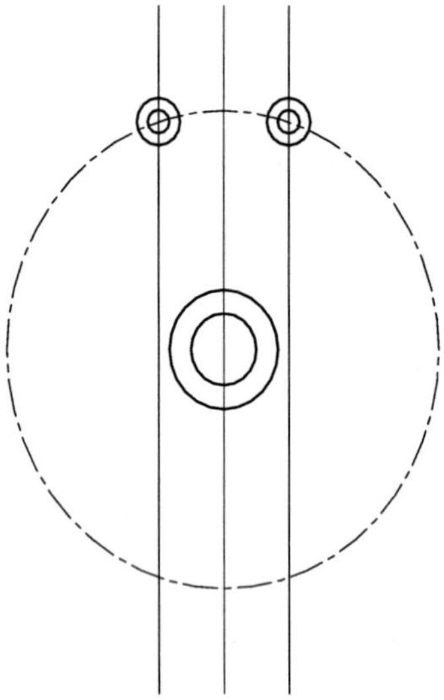

- Erase the two outer construction lines.

- Offset the construction line 7 mm to both sides.

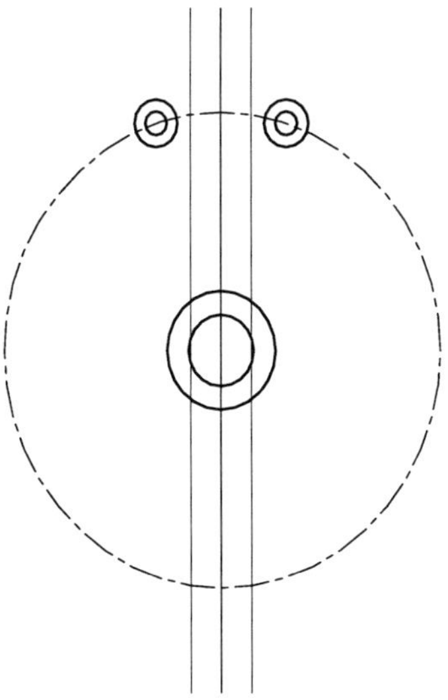

- Draw a line from point 1 to point 2 – in both sides

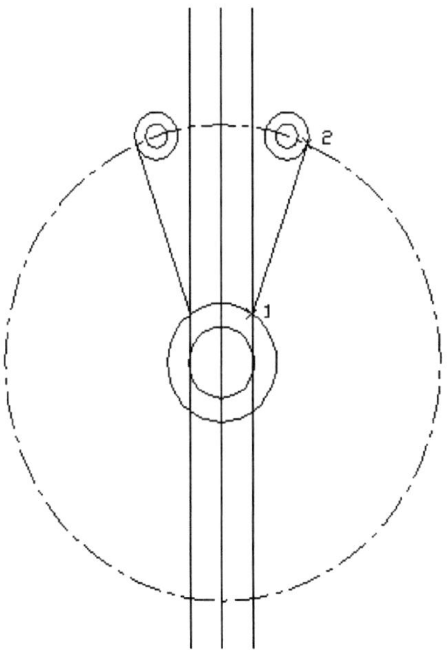

- Draw four concentric circles with radius 45 – 47.5 – 52.5 and 55 units. The circles has the same centre as the two first circles we draw.

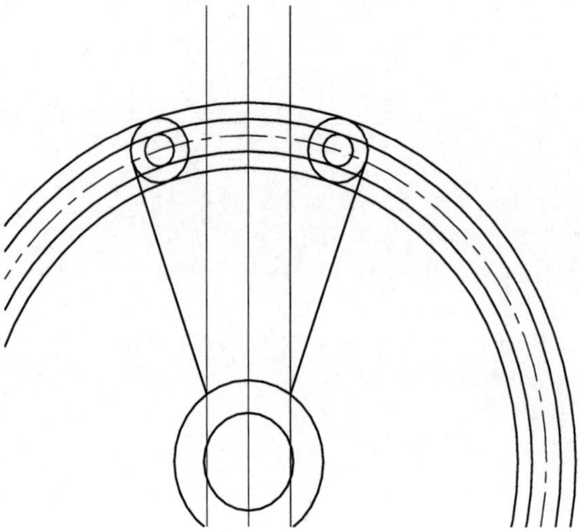

- Remove the construction lines.
- Trim the circles so that the drawing looks like this:

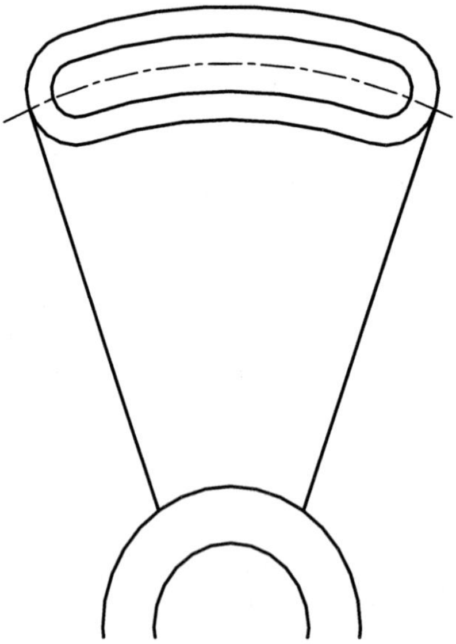

In the drawing the dash-dot line is made longer with the command LENGTHEN.

- Make a FILLET between the circle and the sloping line

In the FILLET command you need to use the subcommand **Trim** and after that you need to use the subcommand **No trim**

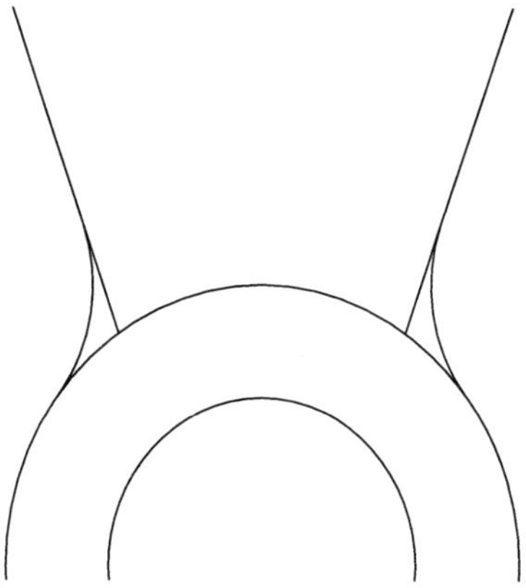

- Dimension the drawing.

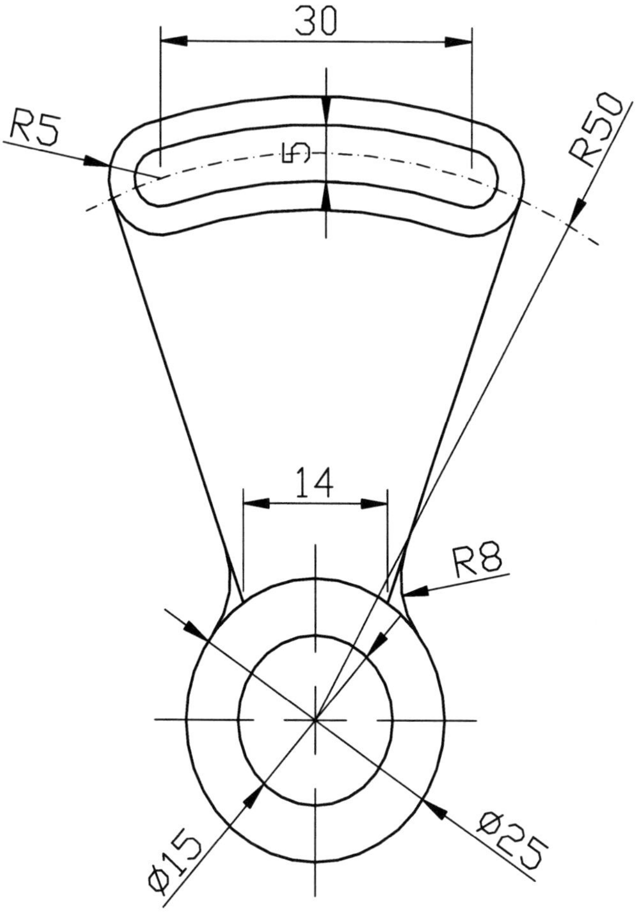

Hub for wind mil

In this exercise we are going to construct a hub to a wind mill. Maybe some of the commands in this exercise will be new to the user. Use the help menu learning these commands.

The drawing should look like this, when you have finished the exercises.

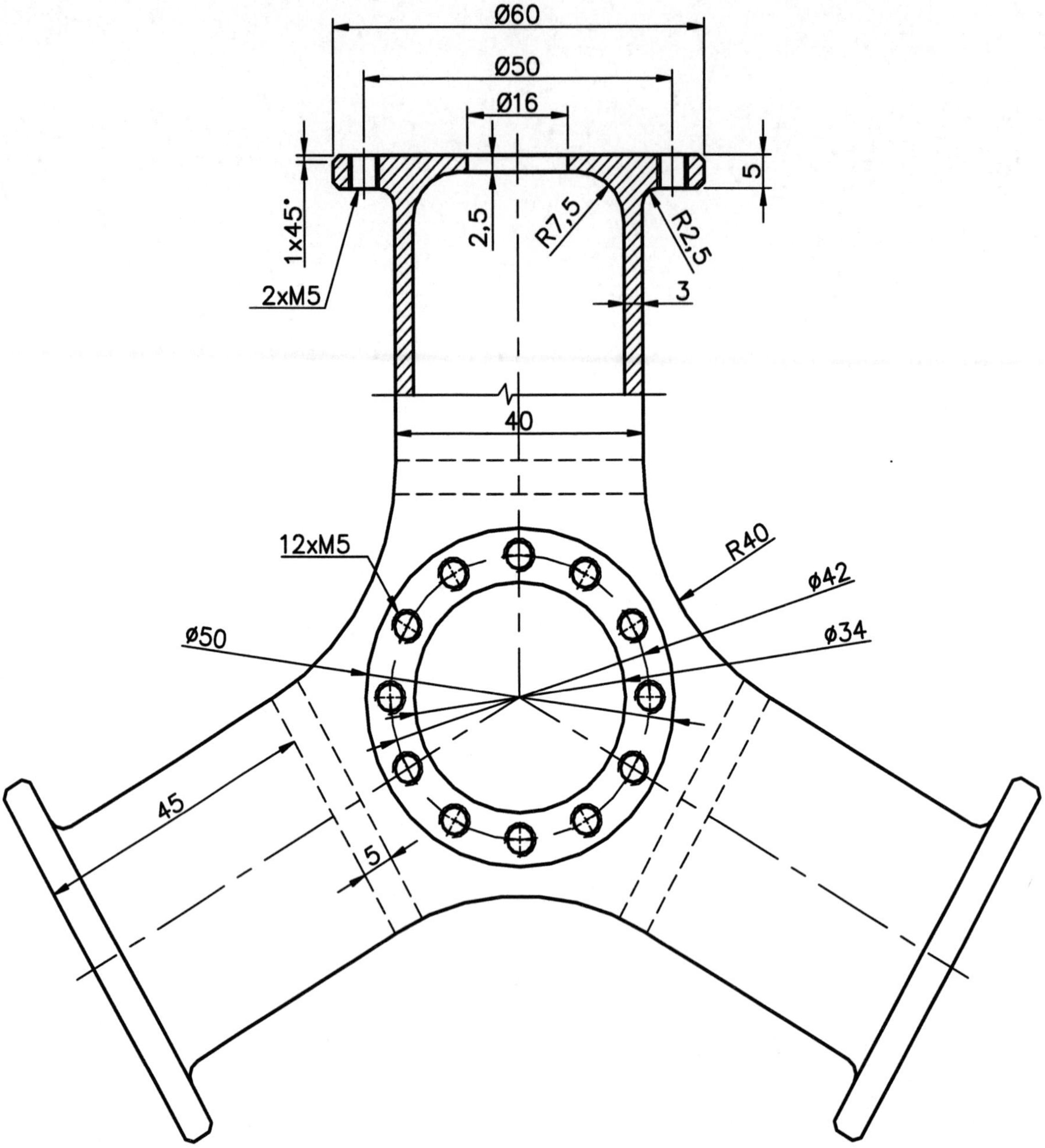

- Change the layer to FRAME
- Draw three concentric circles with the radiuses 25 – 21 – 17.

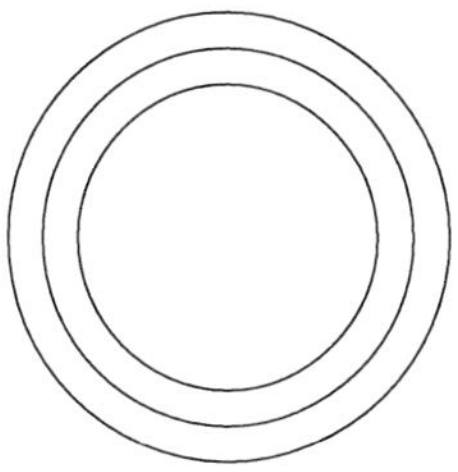

- Draw a line from the centre of the circles and 80 mm vertical.

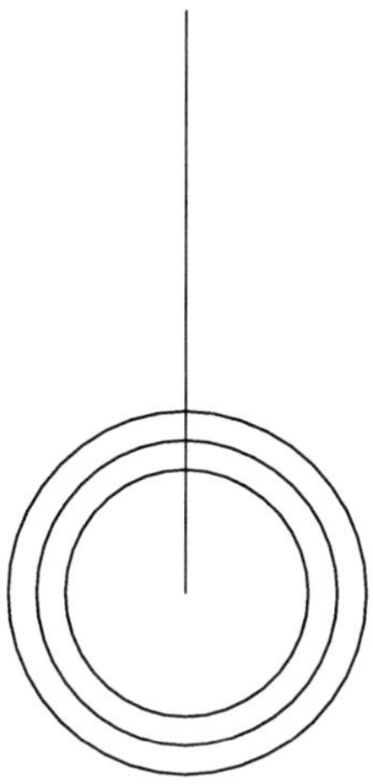

- Offset the line 20 and 30 mm to each side.

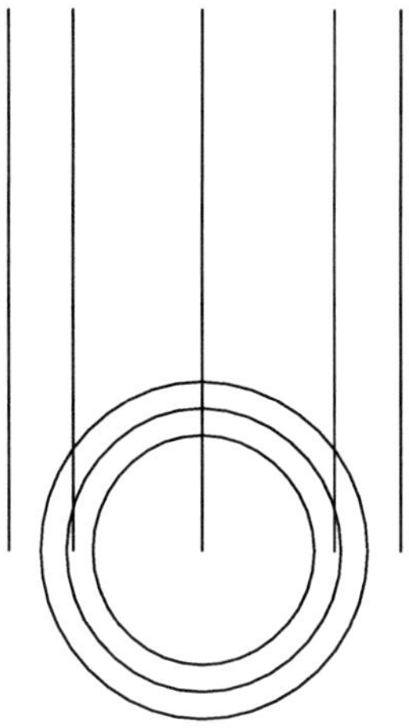

- Draw a line from endpoint to endpoint of the outer lines.

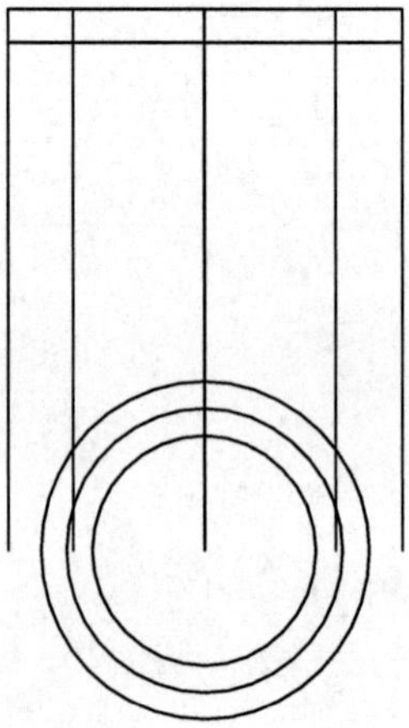

- Use the TRIM, CHAMFER og FILLET commands making the drawing look like the drawing below.

  Chamferdistance = 1
  Filletradius = 2.5

- Move the centre line to layer CENTERLINE so the line is changed to dash/dot. Lengthen the line a bit to the outer side of the horizontal line.

- Offset the upper horizontal line 45 mm vertical down.
- Offset this new line 5 mm vertical down.
- Draw a line horizontal as shown below.

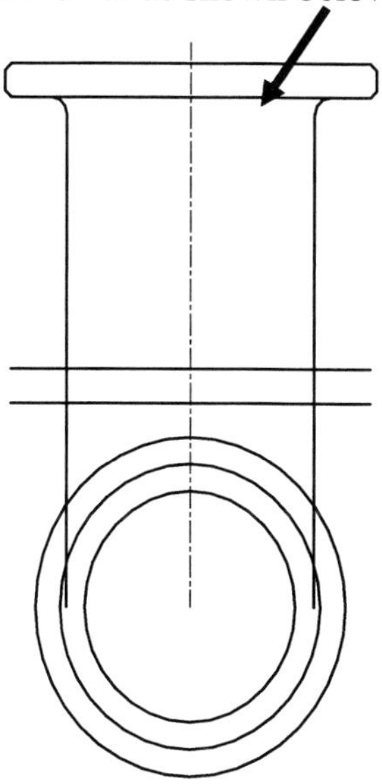

- TRIM the lines so they fit and put them on layer hidden.

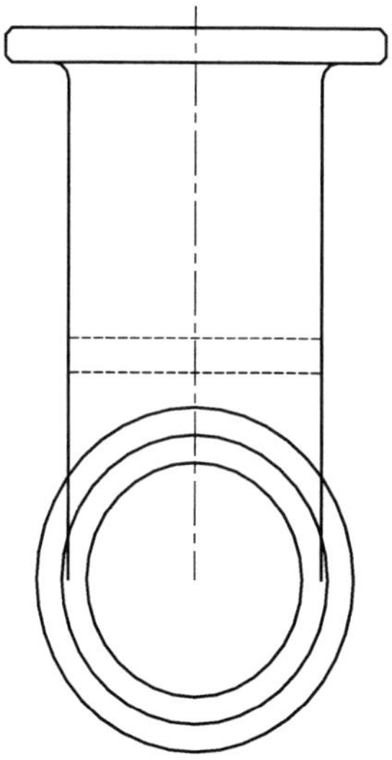

- Make an ARRAY of all the lines

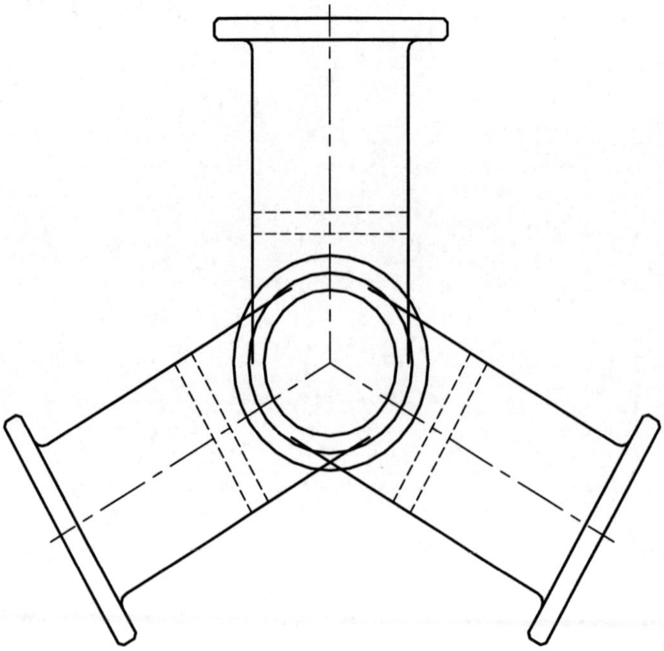

- Make a FILLET between the lines ad shown below Filletradius = 40

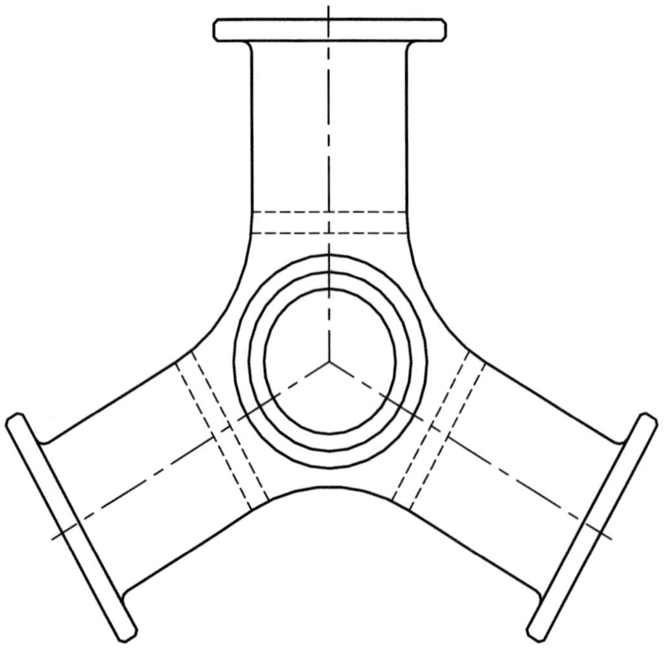

- Draw a ZIG-ZAG line as shown – put the line on a layer called ZIGZAG. You have to construct the line yourself.

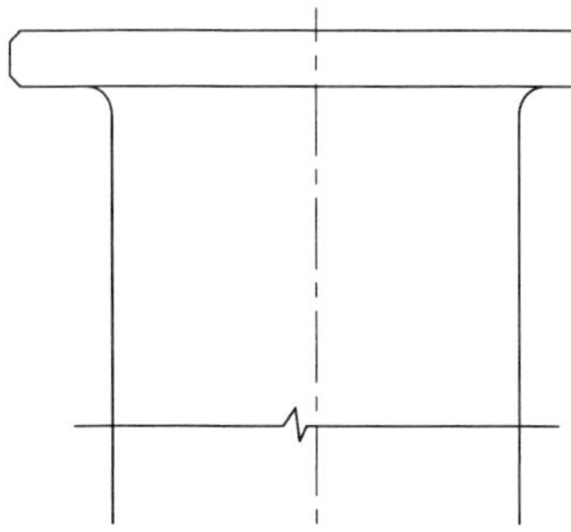

- OFFSET the vertical lines 3 mm inside the others and MOVE the lower horizontal line 2.5 mm up.

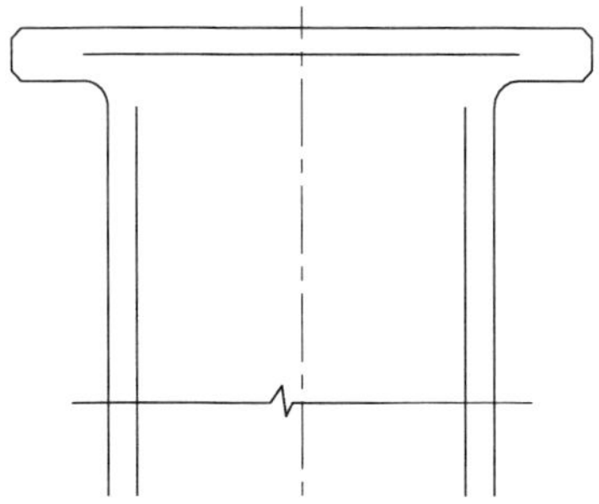

- Make a FILLET on 7.5 mm and TRIM the lines as shown.

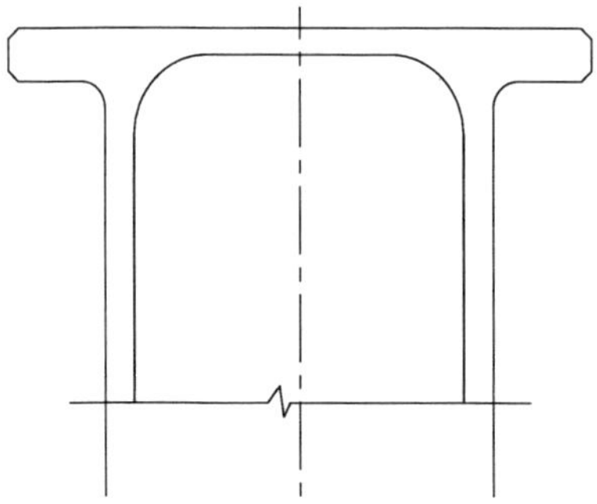

- Draw (use OTRACK) lines in the following distances from the middle line 8 and 25 mm to each side.

- Those lines which are 25 mm from the middle line should be OFFSET 2.5 and 2.05 to each side.

The middle line in the holes we just made shall be on the layer Centerline and shall be lengthen a little bit outside the horizontal lines.

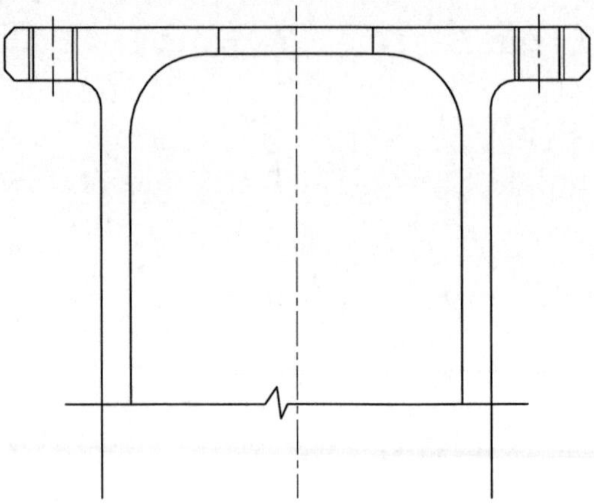

- Hatch the shown areas.

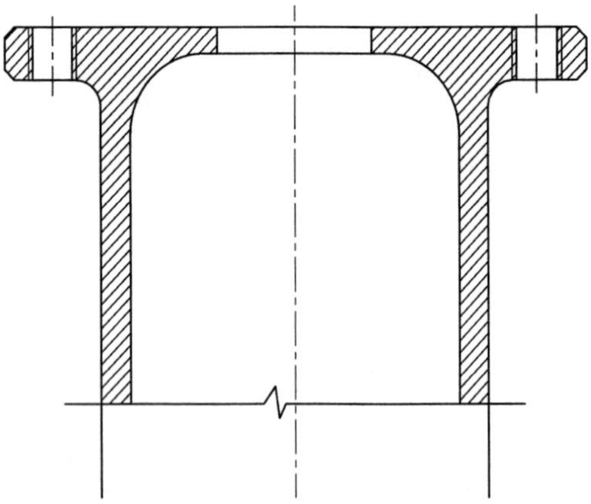

- Move the circle with the radius 21 to the layer Centerline.
- Draw two concentric circles with the radiuses 2.05 and 2.5.
- Cut out a piece of the outer circle as shown.

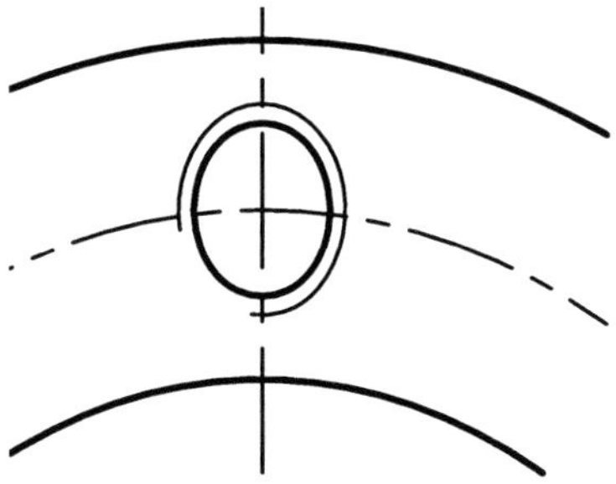

- Make an ARRAY of the screw hole – 12 pieces and they shall not be rotated under the copying.

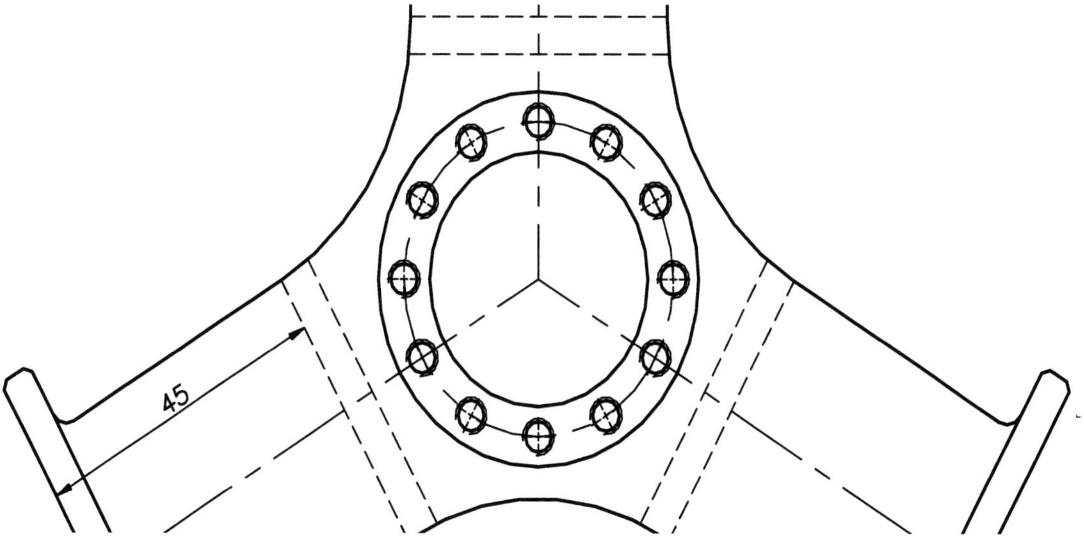

- Dimension the drawing like below.

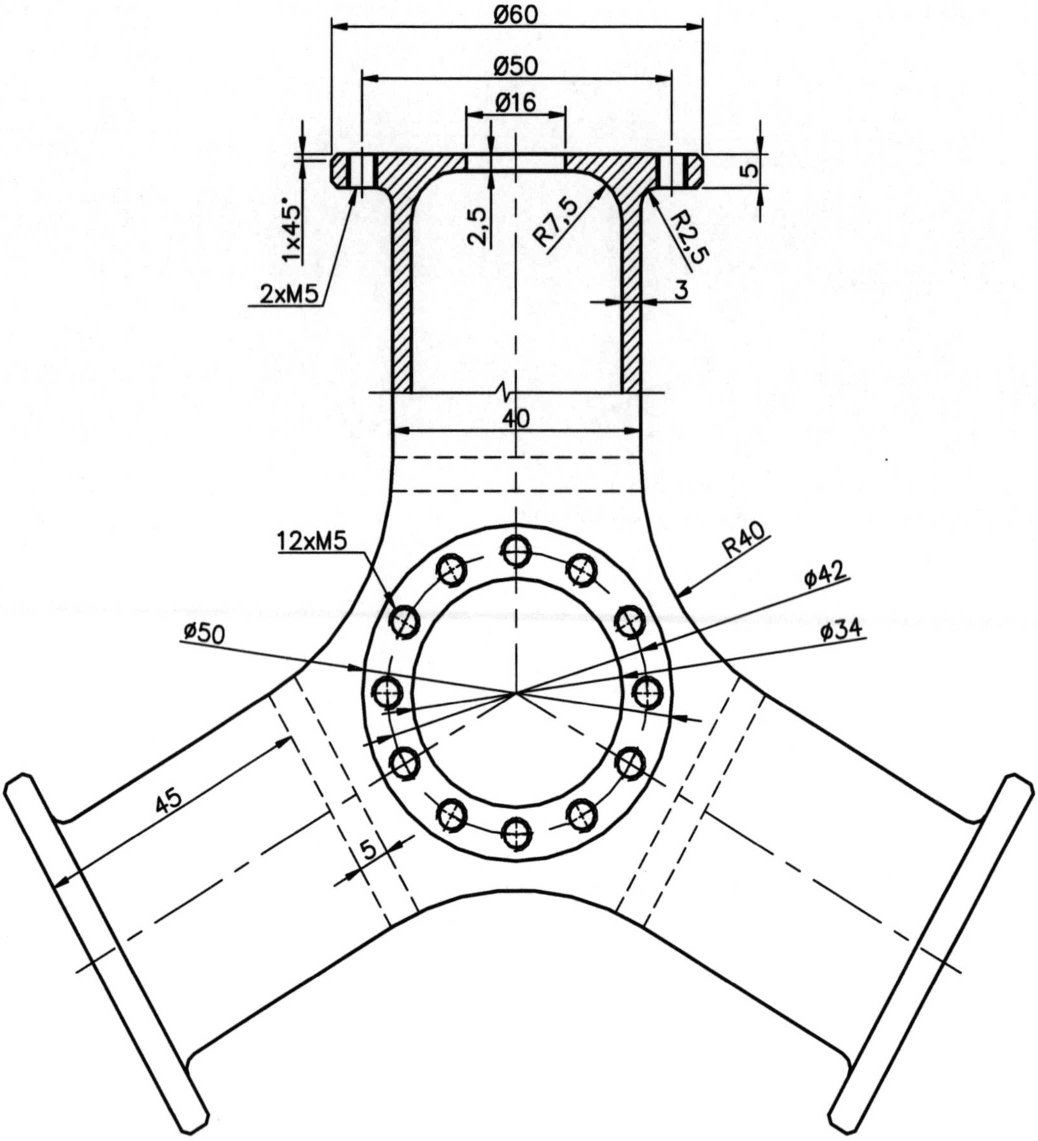